Schools at War

Schools at War

A Story of Education, Evacuation and Endurance
in the Second World War

David Stranack

Phillimore

2005

Published by
PHILLIMORE & CO. LTD,
Shopwyke Manor Barn, Chichester, West Sussex, England

© David Stranack, 2005

ISBN 1 86077 338 9

Printed and bound in Great Britain by
MPG BOOKS LTD
Bodmin, Cornwall

CONTENTS

LIST OF ILLUSTRATIONS

Plates 1-20 can be found between pages 48 and 49

FOREWORD

Roger Moulton, Chairman of AROPS

The Association of Representatives of Old Pupils Societies has carried out a number of surveys over the last thirty years or so, but none has produced information which could be put into book form.

It was in 2001 that Margaret Carter-Pegg and Tim Neale conceived the idea of the Second World War Survey in an attempt to record what had happened to schools during the war. Had the school been evacuated? Had it hosted another school? What had happened to the school premises as a result of the war?

The questions were answered but many AROPS representatives provided a great deal of extra information, and it was very apparent that many schools had fascinating stories to tell. Some schools moved to the other end of the country; some were given a home by other schools; some schools made more than one move; some stayed put and, sadly, one or two closed. There were a great many teachers and pupils who found themselves in situations that they could never have thought possible. Although Edward Gibbon's famous dictum that history is 'little more than the register of the crimes, follies and misfortunes of mankind' is particularly applicable to the story of the Second World War, the stories contained in this book provide many examples of courage, tenacity, determination and an instinct for survival. Indeed, there are many establishments who can claim that their schools actually benefited from their wartime experiences. The AROPS Committee felt very strongly that these experiences should be preserved for posterity and were delighted when David Stranack agreed to write the book.

It is with great pleasure that I commend this book – a new venture for AROPS— in the hope and expectation that it will achieve the wide readership that it undoubtedly deserves.

ROGER MOULTON

Hurstpierpoint
March 2005

Introduction

Six decades on, personal memories of the war years – for those of us who have them – have become dim. I was a little boy living with my family in Bedford. I remember the wail of the air-raid siren as we trooped down the stairs to crawl into the Morrison shelter – a toughened steel cage – that had been assembled in the house's large kitchen. I lay at one end, next to my mother, with my brother on her other side, and then grandfather and grandmother. Father had long since departed to fight the war in some far-flung corner of the world.

And I remember the evacuees from the East End of London who were billeted further down our road, and who introduced a different dimension to the genteel and ordered existence of our quiet Midlands town.

It is almost easy now to look back on those war years benignly. But, of course, I was only a young child and largely unaware of the distress, traumas, upheavals and deprivations with which the grown-ups were having to cope.

Writing this book has made me realise just how extraordinarily different life in the 1940s was for the majority of English people. Families were dismembered, children separated from their parents and sent to live with complete strangers hundreds of miles away, the prospects of sudden death and serious injury were ever present, and mothers waited tensely for the telegram advising them that daddy would not be returning from the war.

The extreme disruption of life is difficult to imagine today, and yet amazingly it was matched by reserves of resilience and fortitude that perhaps the people of England never previously realised they possessed. When in 1940 a German invasion was imminent, and the end of the world as they knew it was nigh, the English showed a remarkable ability to press on regardless. They resorted to humour, and sometimes distracted themselves from the true horrors of war by focusing on the more trivial disadvantages of the conflict. In this book there is more than one tale of schools coping admirably and philosophically with bomb-damaged classrooms and assembly halls without roofs, but when Hitler chose to drop a bomb on the playing fields and Saturday's 1st XV rugby match had to be cancelled, that truly raised the ire of the indignant English.

One cannot help but ponder how England's 21st-century population would cope if they were confronted with similar circumstances today.

The book contains tales of bravery, heroism and commitment to duty that almost defy comprehension. Not this time of soldiers, sailors and airmen, but of headmasters, headmistresses, school teachers and domestic staff who were determined that the education of children would continue, sometimes in ridiculously impossible situations.

The organisation and execution of major evacuations with only a few days' notice, the teaching of classes in the most unlikely improvised accommodation, and becoming surrogate father and mother to unhappy children who had abruptly been separated from their own families, were all part of a teacher's lot in 1939 and the years that followed.

The children reacted in different ways to a world that, for them, had suddenly changed beyond recognition. There was certainly a large number of evacuees who had a miserable war. Over a million children departed from the country's towns and cities in the first week of September 1939. They travelled, sometimes for hours, on crowded trains, not knowing where they were going and, for the younger ones at least, not really understanding why they were going. At their destinations they were marshalled together and assigned to billets in the local houses of complete strangers. Although for some the personalities gelled, and indeed formed the basis for subsequent lifelong loving relationships, for others evacuation was little short of a purgatory in which homesickness became the all-consuming emotion.

Ironically, other children of the war years look back on their evacuations as one of the most idyllic times of their lives. Children from urban environments who were despatched to rural locations often revelled in the greater freedom the countryside offered, and explored with enthusiasm new opportunities that they would never have experienced in town life.

And for many the war was just a great adventure. Children apparently have a remarkable ability to blank out the dangers and the inevitable consequences of armed conflict. For some, the sound of the air-raid siren was eagerly awaited, because leaping out of bed in the middle of the night and scampering down to the shelters was really exciting. The sights and sounds of a German bombing raid on a nearby town were even more exciting, and offered the prospect of collecting pieces of shrapnel the following day. And if you were really lucky there might be a crashed aircraft nearby to provide a whole host of souvenirs before the authorities came to move it away.

Another trend that struck me as I compiled the book was the unfortunate ability of some schools, particularly London ones, always to be in the wrong place at the wrong time. In the summer of 1938, at the time of the Munich Crisis, a declaration of war seemed so imminent that a number of schools decided it was time to put their evacuation plans into operation. No sooner had they arrived at their new destinations than Neville Chamberlain returned from Germany declaring that there would be peace in our time. Within a week or two the evacuation process was put into reverse, and schools returned to their own homes.

It was of course only a year before Hitler's aggressive ambitions once more dominated the scene, and this time there was no last-minute reprieve. England's city dwellers genuinely believed that German attacks from the air would start within hours of war being declared, and the biggest evacuation of people the country had ever experienced was put into operation.

Schools settled into their new homes, sometimes with very makeshift arrangements for both living and teaching, and waited. And nothing happened. The German bombers did not arrive over England, and indeed for the next nine months there were very few signs that the two countries were actually in conflict with one another. It was the time of the Phoney War.

Inevitably, attitudes began to change. Had the evacuation really been necessary? It didn't seem so. Gradually schools took decisions to return to their own homes. Some were away for just a term, moving back during the Christmas holidays, and some waited a little longer. But by the end of the Easter term in 1940 many concluded there was little point in remaining in exile. By the spring of that year a growing sense of security – which was about to be proved wholly false – had persuaded many schools that their original locations were no longer threatened by the dangers of war.

But just as they settled back into what they believed would be their pre-war way of life, Hitler made his move. Within a month Holland, Belgium and France had fallen, and the German war machine was only twenty miles away across the Channel. Invasion was believed to be imminent, and it was the schools in the south-east of England that were most at risk. These included some which had evacuated from London some nine months earlier. At that time, relocation to the comparatively rural counties of Kent and Sussex had seemed a sensible strategy for avoiding the expected air attacks on the capital. Now they were in the front line, and rapidly began planning their second evacuations.

The invasion didn't come. But the Battle of Britain and the Blitz did. Many schools which had drifted back to their own urban homes during the spring of 1940 only remained there for a few months before setting off again. Very often the buildings they had occupied during their first evacuations had by now been requisitioned for war purposes, so the search for new homes had to start again from scratch. It wasn't easy, but gradually the country's towns and cities once more emptied of school children, leaving the adults to cope with the stresses of nightly air raids.

This time evacuations lasted longer. But by 1942 the threat of intensive and sustained enemy action had diminished. Again, there was a drift back to the cities. Sometimes schools were reluctant to return, wary of a possible repeat of the occurrences of 1940. But parents were no longer prepared to be separated from their children, and schools which resisted a return often found that pupil numbers declined to a point at which their financial viability was threatened.

By early 1944 many schools had reoccupied their own premises, sometimes only after protracted battles with the authorities to achieve de-requisitioning. As the D-Day landings proved successful, it seemed that the end of the war was in sight. But Hitler had one more card to play. It was only days after the Allies' invasion of mainland Europe that V1 flying bombs and V2 rockets began to rain on London and other southern cities. Some parts of the capital received a greater battering than they had done in the Blitz. Schools which had just moved back into their buildings after five years in exile were blown apart. The desperation must have been intense.

Fortunately this final fling of the German war machine was relatively short-lived. Hitler's launch pads were overrun by the advancing Allies, and on 8 May 1945 it was all over.

The schools, whether back in their own homes or still away in remote parts of the country, joined with the rest of England in uninhibited and exuberant celebration.

The origins of this book are set out in Roger Moulton's Foreword. It is based entirely on the contributions of Old Pupils' Societies, and their schools, in response to AROPS's original survey and subsequent requests for information. Apart from the occasional exploration of the history pages of schools' websites, I have done no further original research. This is why the book is structured in the way that it is. I have simply summarised and written up the material that has been gathered, in the form of an entry for each contributing society and school. For some schools we only have the barest of facts. Others provided copies of newsletters, articles, reminiscences and complete history books, from which their entries have been culled. Inevitably, for many schools we have no information at all, and so no entries for these appear.

The nature of the book, and the manner of its compilation, has caused its editorial committee to think hard on the subject of references and credits. Over two hundred people have contributed in some form to making this publication possible. To name them all would be difficult, time consuming and prone to error and omission. So we have decided on a single corporate expression of gratitude, rather than an attempt to name everybody individually.

So, to all those old boys, old girls, school archivists, history authors, newsletter writers, reunion organisers and those who just provided their own reminiscences – a big thank you. This is your book.

LIST OF SCHOOLS

Adcote School, Shrewsbury

The advent of war had one immediate and unexpected effect at Adcote – a significant rise in the number of pupils. Families living in areas of the country which were most likely to attract the attentions of the Luftwaffe were desperate to move their children to schools further away from the anticipated dangers, and for many girls Adcote, in the wilds of Shropshire, was the chosen destination.

In 1939 Mrs Gough, the Headmistress, brought forward the start of the Autumn Term to 9 September, but even so many pupils, some of them complete strangers, had started arriving ten days earlier.

Many school activities quickly assumed a wartime flavour. Senior girls attended first-aid classes run by the Red Cross, and learnt about Air Raid Precautions. A make-shift shelter was constructed in the cellars, and there were innumerable problems with blackout – first of all in finding sufficient material to cover all the buildings' windows, and subsequently for both staff and pupils trying to find their way around the school grounds in pitch darkness.

Great efforts were made by the Headmistress and staff to preserve the spirit of the School in spite of the problems and hardships of war. An old girls' reunion was defiantly held as the Blitz began in London in September 1940 and various tales of bravery were recounted. One Old Adcotian had suffered severe injuries, but survived, when the ambulance she was driving was blown up around her, and another ex-pupil had been recommended for the George Cross.

The School was perhaps affected more by the need to respond to the wartime situation than it was by the war itself. Shrewsbury was relatively untouched by the conflict, although the nightly drone of enemy bombers on their lethal sorties to Liverpool and Manchester was a frequent reminder of imminent danger. By 1942 both staff and senior pupils were mounting round-the-clock watches on the school roof in anticipation of the expected German invasion.

Adcote was not immune to the deprivations of war. The domestic staff worked miracles with the declining quality and quantity of food, even though much of the School's grounds had been ploughed up for crop production. Adcotians of the time remember making large quantities of marrow and ginger jam – not universally popular.

The School was nevertheless determined to make its contribution to the war effort. Money was collected and sent to the Spitfire Fund, and the girls adopted a trawler and spent hours knitting sea boot stockings for the fishermen.

1

All forms of paper were in short supply, and the availability of petrol diminished to the point at which matches could only be played against other schools within walking distance. It was not unusual for visitors to arrive on bicycles or even horseback.

Ampleforth College, York

The Junior School within the College looked after pupils from Avisford Preparatory School.

Ardingly College, Sussex

The Headmaster, Canon Crosse, was determined that the College would not be moved. Even so, contingency plans were prepared for an evacuation to Denstone in 1941. During that same year the College was used for some military exercises, and there were rumours that Field Marshal Montgomery was to use it for his headquarters. In the event the evacuation plan was never acted upon, and the Field Marshal failed to appear.

Ashville College, Harrogate

In 1940 the Ministry of Defence requisitioned Ashville's buildings to provide accommodation for Air Ministry staff evacuated from London. The possibility of closing the College altogether for the duration of the war was considered, but there was a real fear that once closed it would never reopen. So a search for a new home in which nearly 200 boys could be educated was initiated, and the *Hydro Hotel* in Bowness, Windermere was the first viable alternative to emerge. As with many other hotels at that time it was for sale, and it certainly fulfilled the requirement of being in a low risk area of the country.

Although the authorities gave the College only twenty four hours to evacuate its buildings in Harrogate, the premises then remained unoccupied for a year, and were in a very poor state of repair when the College eventually returned after the war.

Considering the less than ideal circumstances, Ashville ran remarkably successfully at Windermere during the war years. Sixty years on the College still has strong connections with the area, and holds a reunion for ex-pupils there every year.

Barnard Castle, County Durham

As the war started Barnard Castle announced its willingness to take in any boys whose parents wished to move them away from the primary danger zones. In the event only a relatively small number arrived. To start with, these evacuees were housed in the scout troop's camping facilities, which for the boys was an exciting and popular arrangement.

Barnard Castle was soon confronted with the common problems which affected so many other schools as they adjusted to the changed circumstances of wartime. The teaching staff was rapidly depleted as the younger members joined the armed services. But worthy replacements were found from the ranks of retired masters who returned, perhaps to their surprise, to resume their teaching careers.

Domestic staff also disappeared and the boys found themselves assigned to washing-up duties after meals had been finished in the dining hall. Washing up was not the only new extra-curricular activity. Potato picking for the local farmers and the cultivation of vegetable gardens were embarked upon with enthusiasm. The boys were usually organised into teams based on their houses for these tasks, which provided new opportunities to indulge in inter-house rivalry.

The quantity and quality of food inevitably deteriorated, but it would seem that, at least initially, the boys suffered more in this respect than the staff. This apparent unfairness was uncovered and published in an article by a local paper, and this quickly resulted in a more equitable distribution of food for all.

The School was surrounded by military activity with a number of army and air force bases close by. Good relations were built up with these local units, particularly the South Wales Borderers who took the School under their wing. Sporting fixtures – particularly rugby and cricket – were arranged, and every opportunity was taken to play these matches 'away' as the post-match meals at the military camps were vastly better than the School could provide.

The movement of schools around the country during the war also made new inter-school fixtures possible. Barnard Castle enjoyed playing a rugby match against Mill Hill School, normally nearly 300 miles to the south but evacuated to St Bees in Cumbria just over the Pennines.

Batley Grammar School, Yorkshire

As war broke out Batley took the decision not to relocate. It was not immune, however, to the very different way of life that began to emerge in 1939. That September no school was permitted to reopen for the Autumn Term until adequate air-raid shelters had been provided. Batley was already quite well equipped in this respect, and with some hasty building of additional shelters the School was fully operational by the end of October.

Part of the field next to the school grounds was cultivated for food production, and first-aid classes became a regular feature of school life. Masters and senior boys shared fire-watching duties.

Batley's decision at the beginning of the war to stay put proved in general to be justified, although the School did have one narrow escape. The town of Batley in fact only suffered one air raid throughout the war but the bombs dropped close to the school buildings, causing some damage, and it is reported that the Headmaster, Mr Benstead, and his family were blown off their feet by the force of the explosion.

Bedford School

Bedford town is surrounded by airfields which became RAF bases, and the whole area inevitably attracted the attention of German bombers. Nevertheless, the School decided to remain in situ, and it also became home for the staff and pupils of Victoria College, Jersey who were evacuated from their island.

The links established between the two schools during the war years remain strong to this day. Bedford's preparatory school visits Jersey each Easter Term to compete in inter-school sports, and the Old Bedfordians' Club holds frequent reunions on the island in conjunction with the Old Victorians.

Bedford School also made a cultural contribution to the war effort by making available its Great Hall to the BBC Symphony Orchestra which had been evacuated from London. The orchestra made use of the hall for rehearsals and concerts, many of which were broadcast.

Bedford Modern School

Bedford Modern hosted Dame Alice Owen's School which was evacuated from Islington. Dame Alice Owen's has since moved to Potters Bar.

Benenden School, Cranbrook, Kent

Benenden remained in Cranbrook during 1939 and the first half of 1940, making a contribution to the war effort by taking in and looking after some of the younger boys who were evacuated from Dulwich College Prep School in London.

But by June 1940 air raids and the possibility of invasion made Cranbrook a potentially dangerous place to stay. So Benenden trekked across the country to re-establish itself at the *Hotel Bristol* in Newquay, Cornwall.

Most of the buildings the School left behind in Cranbrook were used as a military hospital for the duration of the war. In August 1944 the hospital was saved from a direct hit by a V1 flying bomb by the bravery of a Free French pilot, Captain Jean Maridor, who was killed in the process.

Leelands Preparatory School at Deal on the Kent coast was even more vulnerable to a cross-Channel invasion. It retreated inland and took up residence in Benenden's vacated New House.

Benenden School returned to occupy its original premises once the war was over.

Berkhamsted School for Girls, Hertfordshire

In July 1939 plans were already being laid for the evacuation of London schools, and Berkhamsted was advised by the government that it would be required to host South Hampstead High School. By the end of the following month schools in London had to be ready to evacuate at a day's notice, and on 1 September Berkhamsted learnt that South Hampstead would be travelling to them by train that same day.

Two days later the Headmistress, 24 staff and 110 girls eventually arrived in a fleet of buses, having been incorrectly routed to Northampton by rail.

Some days after the first arrivals the South Hampstead contingent had grown to 256, many billeted with the families of Berkhamsted pupils.

Berkhamsted welcomed their guests as best they could but in fact their arrival could not have happened at a worse time. A new dining hall and library were under construction – a project that ran from 1938 to 1940 – and the whole School was a building site. Nevertheless, both schools reopened as scheduled on 21 September. Facilities were shared, with Berkhamsted girls working in the mornings, and South Hampstead taking over in the afternoons.

Air-raid shelters had been constructed in the field above the games pitches, and in July 1940 it was reported that '… as a result of many practices the whole school can now reach the shelters within two minutes from the sounding of a whistle or siren'. A year later the boarders' shelters had been improved to the extent that they were heated and lit, and bunks had been installed for the girls' use during night-time air-raid warnings.

The two schools seem to have settled harmoniously into their enforced sharing of Berkhamsted's facilities – no doubt with much goodwill and tolerance from all concerned. There was, nevertheless, a determination on the part of both schools to maintain their separate identities, although they competed with one another on the sports field, and combined for events such as concerts.

On 1 December 1942 there was much excitement when the school was visited by the Prime Minister's wife, Clementine Churchill, herself an old girl of Berkhamsted.

By the summer of 1944 it was deemed safe for South Hampstead to return to the buildings they had vacated five years earlier, and the school said farewell to

Berkhamsted – an event that probably generated mixed feelings of relief and sadness on both sides.

Bloxham School, Banbury

The School remained in situ during the war, but one of their buildings, Palmer House, was requisitioned by the army.

Blundell's School, Tiverton

Blundell's war was typical of many schools fortunate enough to be located in rural England far from the targets of the enemy bombs.

Of course at the start of the hostilities the School prepared for air raids, just as every other school in the country did, regardless of location. Protective trenches were dug and the blackout was rigorously observed. At times the war did not seem too far distant as the glow of fires from Exeter, less than twenty miles away, lit up the night sky. But the School itself only saw a single German bomber. Damaged and probably in difficulties, it flew low over the boarding houses and eventually decided to empty its bomb bays on Tiverton.

Blundell's location in the countryside was attractive to parents wishing to move their children away from the high-risk zones, and there was an immediate influx of new boys from London, Bristol, Plymouth, Cardiff and Swansea. Dover College was also hosted for the Autumn Term in 1940 before it found a home of its own at nearby Poltimore, but cricket and rugby matches between the two schools continued throughout the war. Blundell's sporting standards were also helped by the presence of Hillsbrow, a Surrey prep school which had been evacuated to East Anstey. Hillsbrow was too strong for the local prep schools so played its main fixtures against Blundell's. Many Hillsbrow boys moved on to become Blundellians.

The School also attracted a number of new staff, including several distinguished scholars, who were seeking a more relaxed environment in which to pursue their teaching careers.

Domestic staff, on the other hand, were in short supply. The tradition of eating meals within individual houses soon had to be abandoned and the gymnasium was converted into a central feeding centre, with the boys carrying out many of the domestic chores themselves.

Bradfield College, Reading

Towards the end of 1940 Bradfield began to make its contribution to the war effort.

One of its houses, The Close, was taken over by Claremont, a preparatory school from vulnerable Hove.

Bradfield also provided temporary accommodation for small parties of Londoners such as civil defence workers, firefighters and drivers who needed a short respite from the stress of the blitzed capital. Most of these groups stayed for a week, sleeping in the sanatorium and taking their meals in Hall. There were many who, when they first arrived, dared not walk between buildings without their helmets.

The School also hosted some more unusual refugees. Since 1696 the stone figures of five young scholars – two boys and three girls – had stood above the doors of St Andrew's parish school in Holborn. Fearful that these irreplaceable icons would be destroyed in the bombing, St Andrew's sought a temporary home for them away from London. Bradfield volunteered to become their guardian and the five children were installed safely in the school garden. After the war four of the figures were returned to Holborn, but one of the little girls remained at Bradfield as an offering of thanks from St Andrew's.

Ironically the war also introduced an unexpected element of peace and quiet at Bradfield. In 1940 the college bell was silenced. The order applied to all bells in England which were only to be rung to announce the landing of enemy troops. The result was so peaceful and the inconvenience so minimal that the bell never sounded again.

Bramcote School, Scarborough

As war broke out Bramcote, although it was far from London and the high risk areas of the south east, felt vulnerable. Just over twenty years previously Scarborough town and the School itself had suffered from German coastal bombardment during the First World War.

Opinion was divided, particularly among parents, as to whether the School should evacuate or not, and the issue generated much debate. In the end the decision to go was taken. Fortunately the School had connections with the owner of Eshton Hall at Gargrave near Skipton, and this became its home during the war years.

Bramcote returned to its original buildings in Scarborough when the war was over.

Brighton College

In 1939, as other public schools along the south coast were taking decisions to move to less vulnerable locations, Brighton opted to stand firm and remain at its traditional home. This display of determined steadfastness was not appreciated by all parents, and many pupils, mainly boarders, were withdrawn. The Preparatory School in Sussex Square, and two boarding houses, were closed.

Life quickly became exciting for the remaining boys who were issued with two different identity cards and had to pass barbed wire barricades and armed sentries on their way to and from school.

But the realities of war soon became only too apparent. Enemy planes flying back over the south coast after blitzing London found Brighton a convenient target on which to unload any bombs they had left over. Masters and senior boys, armed with stirrup pumps, water and sand, spent long nights on fire-watch duty. Daytime hit-and-run raiders were also a constant threat, and on one occasion a low-flying enemy plane actually machine-gunned a college cricket match, fortunately without causing any casualties.

By 1942 the College was struggling financially. Pupil numbers had dropped from the pre-war level of 650 to just over one hundred. Additional revenue was desperately needed and eventually an unusual idea was born to help solve the problem. With the help of a parent, George Rushton, who had two sons at the School at the time, the Brighton College Engineering Scheme was set up. The School's engineering workshop was converted into a production unit that was to manufacture parts for wartime munitions. Both staff and boys became involved with this new machine shop, working two-hour shifts at least three times a week. But initially enthusiasm was in much greater evidence than skill. There was a critical day when the factory for which the parts were being made refused to supply any more material to this team of amateur engineers whose end products frequently achieved an 80 per cent rejection rate.

More expertise was sought, the whole system was reorganised and the production line gradually became more efficient. The rejection rate dropped dramatically from 80 per cent to 2 per cent, and this coincided with a rapid and continuous rise in the rate of output. Between September 1942 and July 1943 the team produced 150,000 steel bomb rings, and was entrusted with more difficult work requiring a higher degree of accuracy.

The Brighton College Engineering Scheme continued in operation until 1944, and in the following year the number of pupils at the school had risen again to 350.

Bristol Grammar School

The school remained in its buildings throughout the war and did suffer some bomb damage.

Bromsgrove School, Worcestershire

Planning for the impending conflict started early at Bromsgrove. In December 1938 the then Headmaster, Mr D.J. Walters, received a top-secret letter from a permanent secretary in the Ministry of Works advising him that the School's premises would be requisitioned in the event of war.

The search for alternative accommodation started immediately and by the following summer a deal had been done to take over the *Abernant Hotel* in Llanwrtyd Wells, a remote village in the mountains of Wales.

The formal notice of requisition was issued on 4 September, the day after war was declared. There followed a month of intense planning and feverish activity, and remarkably the School opened in its new home for the Autumn Term on 2 October 1939 with 240 boys. Only 35 had chosen not to make the move.

At first the local Welsh population was somewhat taken aback by the arrival of this English boarding school into its midst, but initial reticence was quickly set aside and the boys and staff were absorbed into the community with kindness and enthusiasm. The school rugby team was particularly well supported.

The dark days of 1940 and the turmoil and upheaval that was being experienced all over England actually created an unexpected opportunity for Bromsgrove. Families were keen to move their children away from the vulnerable urban areas in which many of them lived, and Mr Walters began to be asked by parents if he could take in the younger brothers of some of his existing pupils. The initial handful rapidly grew to a group of over thirty and resulted in a new venture for Bromsgrove, the opening of its first preparatory school.

When the School made its journey to Llanwrtyd Wells in 1939 it was confidently believed that its enforced exile would only last for a year or so. But as 1940 wore on it became obvious that this would not be the case. The School was committed to an existence in Wales for far longer than anyone had originally imagined. After initial success in keeping pupil numbers up, the disadvantage of its new remote location began to become apparent. As senior boys left to join the armed forces the arrival of new boys to replace them diminished to a trickle. Income declined, and the School's deteriorating financial state was not helped by a two-and-a-half-year argument with the authorities over the compensation it was due for its enforced evacuation.

By the spring of 1943 numbers had fallen to subsistence level. Once the leavers had departed at the end of the Summer Term the School would no longer be financially viable. For some time previously the Headmaster and Governors had been attempting to persuade the Ministry of Supply to relinquish at least some of the School's requisitioned buildings in Bromsgrove. With time rapidly running out the prolonged and persistent obstructiveness of civil servants was finally overturned by the Minister himself, and the School's wish was granted.

Bromsgrove reopened on its original site on 28 September 1943 with 147 pupils – a figure which included 43 new boys.

Bruton School for Girls, Somerset

During the war years the School still carried its original name of Sunny Hill School.

In the depths of rural Somerset there was little chance that it would attract the attention of German bombers but in the early months of the conflict all possibilities were considered. Officialdom instructed that all public buildings, including schools, that could easily be identified from the air should be camouflaged. Sunny Hill took the matter seriously and entered into considerable correspondence with various authorities, including the military, as to how the visibility of the School could be reduced. It was pointed out that to camouflage the School fully would be a complex and expensive process, and an alternative of painting all the external walls to blend in with the surrounding countryside was proposed. Just as the School was contemplating whether to use No.5 Ivy Green or No.51 Deep Cement paint officialdom decided its original instructions had perhaps been a bit extreme, and Sunny Hill remained uncamouflaged.

The attitude of Sunny Hill to the war was typical of many rural schools. They became increasingly conscious that they were largely immune to the real dangers and horrors that were being suffered by schools in the commercial and industrial centres of the country. Their determination to compensate for this resulted in almost frenetic efforts to do anything and everything they could to help the war effort.

The girls committed themselves to a minimum of four hours' 'war work' a week. The newly laid tennis courts were ploughed up to provide a potato field before a single set had been played on them, and gradually the School became virtually self-sufficient in vegetables. A frenzy of knitting consumed remarkable amounts of wool – about a hundredweight a year. Each of the four houses adopted one of the services – army, navy, air force and merchant navy – to benefit from their labours, and large quantities of blankets, mittens and other garments were despatched with increasing frequency.

Fund-raising to aid the war effort was addressed with equal enthusiasm. £517 was collected during War Weapons Week in 1941, and a further £711 the following year to support Warship Week.

One of the School's most ambitious projects was mounted in August 1941 when it was converted into a holiday resort for women and children from bombed areas of Bristol. Two parties of about 90 people – ages ranging from 11 weeks to 80 years – were hosted for a fortnight. Sunny Hill old girls who helped out at this event chiefly remember total chaos, enormous gratitude from the guests and a great sense of a worthwhile contribution being made.

The School's ethos of determined contribution to the war effort, combined with its safe location in the country, made it a popular choice for parents, and pupil numbers grew from 195 in 1938 to almost 300 in 1944.

Bryanston School, Blandford, Dorset

The School hosted two prep schools, Dane Court, Pyrford from the autumn of 1939, and Port Regis from the summer of 1940.

Burgess Hill School for Girls, Sussex

It took the retreat from Dunkirk in June 1940 to persuade Burgess Hill that it had become too dangerous to remain in its home a few miles from the south coast.

Arrangements were rapidly made to evacuate the School to the north of England. The Langdale Estate was the chosen location. This had previously been a holiday resort and during the long hot summer the girls enjoyed the freedom of their new rural retreat, sleeping in chalets by a lake and having their meals in what had previously been a tourist restaurant. In fact the weather was so dry that eventually there was insufficient water to maintain adequate standards of sanitation, and outbreaks of sickness and diarrhoea were not uncommon.

Perhaps this was one reason for the Governors to conclude that this long-distance evacuation of the School had not been such a good idea after all. In any event, after only one term at Langdale, the School returned to Burgess Hill and immediately experienced the realities of living in war-torn southern England. Pupil numbers were drastically reduced, and the army requisitioned one of the boarding houses.

But the School's cellars were put to good use. During the Blitz, classes were immediately transferred there if the air-raid siren sounded during the day, and they provided sleeping accommodation for boarders during the night.

Gas masks were carried everywhere, and travelling to school by train, with a gas mask on one shoulder and a satchel on the other, was not a happy experience. The girls became adept at devising schemes to avoid the hated weekly gas-mask practice.

Casterton School, Cumbria

In the depths of rural Westmorland, Casterton remained untouched by the effects of global conflict – apart from the appalling quality of wartime food!

Caterham School, Surrey

Caterham decided to remain in its North Downs location for the duration of the war. In spite of being surrounded by military activity – with the RAF airfield at Kenley and the main Guards Depot being very close at hand – the School managed to function relatively normally, with only an occasional bomb hitting the playing fields.

The indoor swimming pool was required to be kept full at all times in case the water was needed for fire control, but this did not prevent the boys, and also the girls from nearby Eothen School, continuing to use it for its original purpose.

Caterham was considered as a possible host for other schools which had chosen or been forced to evacuate their own premises, but it was decided that its location was already dangerous enough. A request was received, however, for it to accommodate three girl pupils, which in those days caused quite a stir in a boys' boarding school.

Channing School, Highgate, London

Channing realised at an early stage that, in the event of war, evacuation from its London home would be essential. Cornwall, Devon, Wiltshire, Shropshire and Wales were all scoured for suitable locations, and eventually it was decided that Ross-on-Wye offered the best solution. A practice evacuation drill was actually carried out during 1938, when four hotels were used. When the time came for the real thing a year later about 100 girls set off from Highgate and on arrival in Ross managed to squeeze themselves into just two hotels – *The Chase*, and the *Wye* in which the Junior School was accommodated.

The evacuation struck at the very roots of Channing. Moving to unfamiliar and not entirely suitable premises in a country town on the other side of England was bad enough. But the realisation dawned that many of the School's traditions and routines had been inexorably linked to the old familiar buildings it had occupied since 1885. There was a period of unease and disorientation before the School began to re-establish itself in its new environment.

The attitudes of the girls to this new world varied widely. Some were distressed by homesickness, separation from their families, fear of the unknown and the possible dangers of war. Others revelled in the pleasures of a new-found freedom and the delights of the Herefordshire countryside, with long cycle rides, picnic teas and bathing in the river contributing to their enhanced quality of life.

But even for the most sanguine there were hardships to bear. Channing's first winter in Ross was one of the coldest on record. With central heating still very much a luxury that certainly did not extend to the *The Chase Hotel*, not only the water pipes, but the tanks themselves froze. In addition to the constant battle to keep one's blood circulating, buckets of drinking water had to be imported from the nursing home across the road.

Ross was far removed from any wartime action, but in 1940 it was briefly touched by the reality of conflict when, after the escape from Dunkirk, a dishevelled and exhausted contingent of the British Expeditionary Force arrived in the town seeking temporary accommodation.

Three years later the worldwide battle had swung in favour of the Allies, and Ross seemed to be filled with American GIs preparing for the invasion of Europe. The Yanks had no hesitation in showing their interest in Channing sixth-formers, and the more adventurous girls were more than happy to reciprocate.

Christ's Hospital, Horsham

Christ's Hospital remained at Horsham throughout the war. It was not required to host any other schools but did provide accommodation for Canadian troops in the run up to D-Day and as a result was inspected by Field Marshal Montgomery, an event which caused very considerable excitement.

Churcher's College, Petersfield

The College hosted the boys of Emanuel School in London from September 1939 to the autumn of 1945.

City of London School

The School started planning for a possible evacuation in 1938. Marlborough College responded positively to City of London's tentative approach and generously agreed to share its facilities if the need arose. The organisation of the evacuation was thought through in great detail, but its execution was not without hitches. In particular, on 1 September 1939 the officials of the Great Western Railway were stressed by the need to move a huge number of children out of London almost simultaneously, and insisted on loading the CLS contingent on to a train travelling non-stop to Taunton.

Prolonged negotiations with the driver eventually resulted in the train making an unscheduled stop at Marlborough.

The sharing of a single location by a London day school and one of the country's leading public boarding schools was not the easiest situation to manage successfully. The attitudes, traditions and working practices of the two establishments differed widely.

A detailed and complex plan was created to enable the two schools to use Marlborough's facilities independently of one another. Initial scepticism in some quarters that it could never work proved unfounded. It did. There was a degree of grumbling and unhappiness, but this was largely outweighed by a great deal of goodwill from the majority, and a preparedness to compromise.

Many CLS boys were at first taken aback by the sudden move from their familiar urban environment into a distinctly unfamiliar rural world. The countryside lacked the entertainment options of town and was deemed to be boring. Only gradually were eyes opened to the different pleasures of the Wiltshire downs, Savernake forest and the Kennet valley. Inevitably there were some London exiles who refused to be impressed by their new surroundings, and the staff went to considerable lengths to find new ways of maintaining interest and enthusiasm. A number of new clubs and societies were born during the Marlborough years including a Railway Club and an Aircraft Spotters Club. The members of the latter became adept at identifying the occasional German Heinkel bomber which strayed from time to time over the English countryside.

Although housed in the relative safety of Wiltshire, the boys of CLS were never completely immune from the tragedies of war. One Citizen of the time remembers his friend being called out of class by a grim-faced master one morning to be told in private that both his parents had been killed in an air raid the night before.

As the war wore on CLS was threatened more by diminishing pupil numbers than by enemy action. By 1942 the dangers of living in London were apparently abating and a growing number of parents was inclined to retrieve their children from the remote countryside. The number of pupils had dropped to 500, the lowest since 1845. By the end of the Spring Term in 1944 the number was down to 430, compared with Marlborough's 700, and it was at this point that CLS took the decision to return to London.

City of London School for Girls

As the prospect of conflict grew closer the School's location in the heart of London could not have been more vulnerable. In fact the Headmistress, Miss Winters, was advised as early as September 1938 that evacuation would be inevitable should war be declared. During the early months of 1939 contingency plans were made to share the premises of the City of London Freemen's boys' school in Ashtead, Surrey.

The evacuation duly occurred that September, with girls being billeted in the homes of families who lived in the Ashtead area.

The arrangement with City Freemen's was that the boys would make use of their school buildings during the mornings, and the girls would move in for the afternoons. This segregation of the sexes was so effective that the CLSG girls who experienced it can barely remember a boy ever being seen!

The Green Roof Tea Room on Ashtead Common, a building that is remembered so clearly to this day by those who were evacuated, was requisitioned as an administrative base for the School. The Headmistress and her secretary established an office there, and the girls used the building in the mornings for various activities and for lunch, before walking the mile to City Freemen's in a crocodile.

In March 1940, after six months of Phoney War, people were beginning to wonder what all the fuss had been about, and there was even talk of the School returning to its home in Carmelite Street, London. Two months later the German invasion of the Low Countries and the escape from Dunkirk abruptly put an end to such thinking.

As the situation grew even worse with the start of the Blitz, it became clear that Ashtead was almost as dangerous a place to be in as central London. It was clear that the school would have to move again, and this time further afield. The countrywide search for a new home ended in Keighley, Yorkshire. Here CLSG would share the premises of the boys' Junior Technical School, with science lessons being held at Keighley Girls Grammar School.

It was the end of October 1940 before this second evacuation could be organised, causing a very late start to the Autumn Term. Many of the girls travelling by train from Kings Cross were about to experience life in northern England for the first time – in those days a marked contrast to life in the south. For the second time in just over a year the girls were confronted again with the prospect of being billeted with complete strangers in an unknown town. Some billeting arrangements worked well from the start with the new guest being absorbed into the heart of a family and establishing a relationship that lasted a lifetime. Others were not so lucky and there were many tales of unhappiness and homesickness.

CLSG remained in Yorkshire for three years, eventually returning to its London home in 1943. As with so many other evacuated schools, pupil numbers suffered. There were 172 girls at the School in Keighley at the end of the Autumn Term in 1940. But on the School's return to its original buildings in Carmelite Street this figure had dropped to about one hundred.

Clifton College, Bristol

During the early months of the war the College felt safe in its location far from London and the south east. But by the summer of 1940 cities all over the country were being subjected to the German bombing Blitz, and Bristol was certainly not immune.

On the night of 24 November 1940 the city suffered a devastating attack in which 200 people were killed and 900 injured, and the College Governors decided that evacuation could no longer be delayed. But by then many other schools had already taken this step and finding an available building in the countryside large enough to house the whole College was an almost impossible task. The prep school was packed off to Butcombe Court in Somerset, and it was the army that eventually provided a solution for the senior school. Some hotel buildings in Bude, Cornwall which the military had already requisitioned were offered to the College in exchange for use of its own buildings in Clifton.

So the deal was done. By February 1941 the boys of Clifton were enjoying their exile by the Cornish seaside, while the College's home became the base for many of the American army's headquarters staff.

While the Americans were in residence, the College was graced with a royal visit. Queen Mary asked to see a game of baseball, having been introduced to the sport during the First World War. Two teams were hastily organised, a pitch marked out on the Close, and the royal wish was granted.

The most senior American soldier to have offices at the College was General Omar Bradley who was in charge of the US First Army. Bradley arrived in October 1943 and established himself in the Housemaster's drawing room in School House. During the next few months many of the plans for the Allies' D-Day invasion of France were developed and refined in Clifton's buildings.

In 1949 General Bradley was made an honorary Old Cliftonian and he revisited the College in 1953 when he represented President Eisenhower at the Queen's coronation. It was on that occasion that he asked that the Stars and Stripes should be flown from the College tower each 4 July – and it has done ever since.

The College eventually returned to Bristol in March 1945. Life in Cornwall had been very different but apparently not without its academic successes. On at least one occasion during its exile the College achieved top place in the list of Oxbridge scholarships.

Clifton High School, Bristol

As with Clifton College it was early in 1941 before the realities of war had to be faced.

It was decided in January of that year not to evacuate the School itself but to find less vulnerable accommodation for its boarders. The School was indeed fortunate when Lady Wraxall offered to make available her splendid Victorian mansion at Tyntesfield some five miles from Bristol – a property that has subsequently been acquired by the National Trust.

The Headmistress and another member of staff established themselves at Tyntesfield and organised accommodation for the boarders there. The girls were bussed into Clifton in the morning and returned to their rather exotic new home at the end of the school day. Day girls continued to attend the School as usual.

The use of Tyntesfield continued until July 1945.

Colet Court (St Paul's Junior School), Hammersmith, London

Before the war Colet Court was an independent preparatory school which had a close association with St Paul's School. It had in fact been founded in 1881 at the suggestion of St Paul's High Master. The majority of Colet Court boys progressed on to become Paulines.

The Munich Crisis of 1938 precipitated the School's first brief evacuation to Bigwood Camp near Radley. But after two weeks, with world peace apparently restored, Colet Court returned to its own London premises.

A year later most pupils evacuated to Bigwood for a second time, although a small number of boys remained at the School in London. Accommodation was also arranged for about 40 boarders at Danesfield, a large recently modernised house at Medmenham near Marlow.

The occupation of both these locations was short-lived. Bigwood Camp was just not suitable for a long-term stay, and the contingent of boys from there was taken in by Radley College. Then in January 1941 the boys at Danesfield were confronted with a further move when the building was requisitioned by the RAF. Canford School in Dorset initially came to the rescue with the offer of one of its houses which included dormitories, classrooms and the use of a sanatorium. But unfortunately the Canford

Governors decided that the house must be closed, and the boys were on the move again. Their next stop was Wellesley House at Wellington College. The College had actually put this house at the disposal of St Paul's School, and the then High Master of St Paul's, Walter Oakeshott, made it available to Colet Court.

Throughout the war a branch of Colet Court remained open in London. Its main building was requisitioned early on by the Royal Army Medical Corps Records Department, and the School moved for a time into its own boarding house. From 1941 onwards the number of pupils began to increase as families felt it was safe to bring their children back to London, and further moves were made to Colet Girls' School, the prep school of St Paul's Girls, and then Colet House, one of the boarding houses at St Paul's.

In 1943 Colet Court's previous close relationship with St Paul's was finally consummated when it officially became St Paul's Junior School.

The School's final out-of-town location was Easthampstead Park, a large mansion near Crowthorne in Berkshire which had been used by St Paul's for most of the war. When the senior school returned to London in 1945, Colet Court moved in and remained at Easthampstead until the autumn of 1946, when at long last the whole School was reunited in its original Hammersmith home.

Commonweal Lodge School, Purley (now The Lodge School)

Commonweal was relatively unaffected by the war until the autumn of 1940. The army then decided that the School's buildings were essential to its purpose, and took them over. The School only managed to survive in the short term through the kindness of an old girl who lived in a large house nearby and made three of her rooms available for the few remaining pupils to continue their classes.

In early 1941 it was decided that the School must move away from the London area. Miss Bray, the Headmistress and one of the founders, had heard of a new school that had recently opened in Lewdown, Devon, and arrangements were made for Commonweal's remaining 25 girls to be transferred there. The move was a success and by the following summer the number of pupils had risen to forty. Ardock, the house in which the School was accommodated, had to be extended to cope with the extra activity.

Rural Devon was a different world from the suburbs of outer London, and the Commonweal girls were not slow to enjoy the new opportunities it offered. Vegetables were cultivated to help with the war effort and the school acquired two cows to ensure a constant supply of milk. Horse riding and country dancing became popular extra-curricular activities. But academic learning was not neglected and several girls took their School Certificate while they were in Devon.

Nevertheless, the desire to return to the School's original home in Purley was never far beneath the surface, and in 1943 after two years in Devon the decision was taken to go back. The army was still in occupation of the main building, but the School was allowed to use one of the subsidiary buildings on the site. Commonweal reopened with a mere 20 pupils, but this number rose rapidly to 60 who could barely be squeezed into the cramped quarters.

The army eventually departed in 1945 and it was with much pleasure and relief – and after a lot of cleaning and repairs – that Commonweal was finally re-established in the premises that had been built for it almost 30 years previously.

Convent of the Sacred Heart, Roehampton (now Woldingham School)

At the end of August 1939 the Sacred Heart's Community of nuns was attending its annual retreat. On 1 September the news was so ominous that the retreat was cut short, and the nuns returned to the Convent at Roehampton in south west London, to prepare for evacuation.

The removal to Newquay in Cornwall had already been planned, and on Sunday the 3rd an advance party set off from London for the West Country in a convoy of coaches and cars. As they passed Basingstoke the news came through that the country was at war.

The evacuees eventually arrived at the *Hotel Marina* late in the evening, only to find that it was barely fit for habitation. For the next few weeks the nuns worked tirelessly at cleaning and organising, while the girls could not believe their luck to be finishing their extended summer holiday at the seaside in glorious weather.

The evacuation thrust the nuns into a totally new and unfamiliar world. The private, secluded and ordered life of the Convent was gone. Suddenly they were part of a secular and very public community. The transition must have been traumatic. But they rose to the occasion, and most subsequently acknowledged that it had been a 'character forming' experience.

By the end of September the whole Convent had gathered in Newquay and the Autumn Term had started. But three months on it became clear that it would not be possible for the School to see out the war on the north Cornish coast. Beaches were being mined, coastal defences built and eventually the *Hotel Marina* itself was requisitioned by the army.

At Easter 1940 Stanford Hall in Leicestershire, a magnificent 17th-century country mansion owned by Lord and Lady Braye, became the Convent's second wartime home. The Brayes, recognising that the Hall would undoubtedly be required to make its own contribution to the war effort, felt that making it available to the Community of the Sacred Heart was a more attractive proposition than having it requisitioned by the military.

Stanford Hall with its beautiful rooms and corridors furnished with priceless antiques and other treasures could not have been more different from the *Hotel Marina*. Nevertheless, a degree of ingenuity was still required to convert this stately home into a working convent school.

The Sacred Heart remained at Stanford Hall for six years. Although the improvised teaching and living accommodation was far from ideal, the Convent managed to maintain high academic standards throughout, and there is no doubt that the wartime generation of girls enjoyed the Hall's glorious grounds and the surrounding countryside to the full.

While the Convent flourished in Leicestershire, its original buildings in Roehampton were progressively damaged and eventually destroyed by bombs during the autumn of 1940.

In 1946 a new home – Marden Park – was acquired in Woldingham, Surrey, and after a summer of building work and removals the Convent reopened there at the start of the Autumn Term.

Cranleigh School, Surrey

The summer months of 1939 saw Cranleigh responding to the government's instructions to prepare for war. Trenches were dug and sandbags installed to provide protection during air raids, and a variety of blackout arrangements created. But perhaps the biggest change to the School's pre-war routine came from the arrival in its midst of the boys from Carn Brae Preparatory School.

Carn Brae's location in the London borough of Bromley made its early evacuation inevitable. The headmasters of the two schools knew each other well and they had previously come to an informal agreement that Cranleigh would host the prep school should the need arise. Arrangements were made during the summer holidays for Carn Brae's departure from Bromley – which subsequently came to be one of the most bomb-damaged areas of London – and its arrival at Cranleigh for the start of the Autumn Term. The absorption of the younger boys into Cranleigh's way of life went remarkably well, and the two schools worked harmoniously together until Carn Brae's eventual return to London in March 1946.

Cranleigh contributed enthusiastically to the war effort. A huge fête in the Summer Term of 1940 raised one hundred guineas for the Red Cross. Large areas of the school grounds were cultivated to grow crops and vegetables, and the lawns were left uncut to be harvested for hay.

The war suddenly became more threatening and personal when German radio announced specific plans to bomb England's public schools. Eton, Harrow and Ardingly had already been targeted, and there was a wild rumour that Cranleigh would be next. On this occasion the rumour was either too wild or the German bombers were too inaccurate, for the School failed to receive the anticipated attention.

But war was all around. The air-raid siren seemed to sound continuously, enemy bombers droned overhead every night, the sight of aerial dogfights became almost commonplace, and inevitably the first stick of bombs dropped in the school grounds. Fortunately these ones were small and did no damage.

Gradually England's air defences grew stronger and the threat of sudden death from the skies diminished, albeit temporarily. For 1944 was the year of the flying bomb. Once again Cranleigh was in the thick of it, and serious consideration was given to the possibility of evacuation, even at this late stage of the war. The decision was taken to stay and the School's somewhat unusual and frequently interrupted life continued. On one occasion pupils sitting a School Certificate exam were ordered to break off from their writing and shelter under their desks until a flying bomb had passed.

The nearest to a direct hit came after the School had broken up for the summer holidays in 1944. A flying bomb landed in the school grounds early one morning showering the Headmaster, who was still in bed, with plaster and causing damage to a number of buildings, fortunately none of it too serious.

Croham Hurst School, South Croydon

Miss Humphrey, Croham Hurst's Headmistress, made an early start to planning the School's possible evacuation from the London area. In 1938 she located and leased a large mansion called Bridge House at South Petherton in Somerset. By September that year the political situation in Europe was looking ominous and war seemed imminent. A precautionary decision was taken to evacuate part of the School, some 60 girls. They did not remain long. The Munich agreement was signed and after only two weeks the girls returned to Croydon.

Nevertheless, the experience gained from this trial run proved useful when the time came for a more major evacuation a year later. By then Bridge House had been made more habitable. It had even had central heating installed as a result of one pupil's father, an engineer, removing all the radiators from the Croydon building and refitting them in the School's new home.

Almost immediately Croham Hurst found itself hosting in its new premises another group of evacuated children from the Hall School in Weybridge. The accounts of those who experienced this period of cohabitation suggest that the two schools had widely differing cultures and were less than compatible. Perhaps this was why the sharing arrangement only lasted for one term before the Hall moved away to a new location in Wincanton.

Life in the country was safer, but there was no escaping the fact that Britain was at war. German bombers could be heard overhead on their way to attack Bristol. There were fire-watching duties to be fulfilled and sleep was constantly disrupted by night-time excursions to the air-raid shelters in the cellars.

But by 1942 the dangers of the conflict seemed to be diminishing and some parents were becoming keen for their girls to return home. So it was decided to re-establish a Croydon base for Croham Hurst. The School's main buildings had been leased as offices to an insurance company that believed it would be safer in suburbia than central London. But a subsidiary building, the Tower House, was available and the 'Croydon Branch' of Croham Hurst was reopened there with just 10 pupils.

The logistics of running two schools 100 miles apart were not easy. Several members of staff had teaching responsibilities at both locations and spent much of their time criss-crossing the country by train. Eventually the number of pupils in Croydon grew to the point at which the Tower House was self supporting, and staff commuting was gratefully discontinued.

By the end of the war the School had over 100 pupils in Croydon, and just under 100 at South Petherton. Croham Hurst's evacuation to Somerset came to an end in the summer of 1945. By the start of the following Autumn Term all pupils were back at school in Croydon, and this included a number of Somerset girls who had joined as 'locals' and who finished their education as boarders in the London suburbs.

Croydon High School

Uncertainty surrounded the School's evacuation plans during the summer of 1939. Guidance was sought from the Local Education Authority which seemed to be in two minds as to whether evacuation should be compulsory or optional. Eventually a decision to depart was taken, heavily influenced by the lack of sufficient air-raid shelters at the School's site.

It was not possible to find a new home of sufficient size and capacity to accommodate the whole School, so the girls of Croydon High found themselves scattered around a variety of locations in southern England.

A handful went to Bideford in Devon, and a much larger group to Eastbourne where initially they made use of Eastbourne High School's facilities. The girls were billeted in local homes and part of the *Wilmington Hotel*, but subsequently they moved on to share the facilities of Boston House, a large local private school. By 1940 the Eastbourne exiles had reduced in number from an original 136 to a mere 70, and it was decided to move on again, away from the dangerous south coast, to Llandilo in Wales.

Some girls remained in Croydon and at first worked on assignments at home with teachers visiting. Three rooms were then obtained at a preparatory school in nearby

Sanderstead where the girls worked in relays with the overflow having lessons in staff cars parked at the gate. Matters improved after a couple of months when the old unused buildings of Purley County School were reopened to provide accommodation for Croydon High and two other local schools.

By 1942 the loss of pupils from the two outposts, Purley and Llandilo, was beginning to undermine their financial viability and both were eventually closed.

Meanwhile back in Croydon, with air-raid protection on the site substantially improved, numbers were increasing again, and at prize-giving in the summer term of 1942 the Chairman of Governors spoke of 'our great good fortune in being re-united as one School under one roof'.

The euphoria was of course short-lived. Two years on London and the south east were suffering the brunt of the flying bomb attacks and the school buildings were damaged on a number of occasions. A second exodus from Croydon commenced and many girls sat their School Certificate exams that year in places such as Reading, Oxford and Burnham-on-Sea.

Throughout the years of fighting the girls of Croydon High School were as dedicated as any in their contributions to the war effort. In the Spring Term of 1940 the School adopted the minesweeper, HMS *Snaefell*. The vessel took part in the retreat from Dunkirk and a great variety of gifts for the crew were collected and regular parcels sent off from the School. There was great sadness when the ship was sunk by enemy action on 10 July 1941 with the loss of the captain, Lieut Cdr Brett, and two members of the crew. In the latter years of the war two further Royal Naval vessels, HMS *Laguna Belle* and HMS *Jeanie Deans*, benefited from the girls' efforts.

Cumnor House School, South Croydon

Cumnor House's wartime experiences are interesting in that they resulted in the existence today of two schools with the same name in different parts of the country.

The original School was opened in South Croydon in 1931. Nine years later its proximity to Croydon airport – a prime target for German bombs – made evacuation inevitable, and new premises were found at Danehill in Sussex.

At the end of the war there was some enthusiasm for the School remaining at Danehill, where it does indeed still exist today as a thriving prep school. But others wanted Cumnor House to be re-established in Croydon. So a new school, with the same name, was opened in 1946, which also flourishes today.

Dame Alice Owen's School, Potters Bar

At the beginning of the war the School was located in Islington and was given firm instructions by the government and the London County Council to evacuate to a site at least 50 miles away from the capital.

Bedford Modern School was prepared to act as hosts and the move was made on 1 September 1939.

The School successfully maintained its identity while in exile and returned to London at the end of the war with more pupils than it had when it left.

Dauntsey's School, Devizes, Wiltshire

With a peaceful location in the heart of Wiltshire Dauntsey's did not feel itself in danger from the hostilities of war. In fact the School provided a safe haven briefly for a prep school that had been evacuated from Brighton. It also benefited during the early 1940s from quite a rapid rise in pupil numbers as parents sought places for their children at schools away from the areas of high risk.

The war did nevertheless affect life at Dauntsey's in a variety of ways. The huge wrought iron gates at the School's entrance were the first to go. They were quickly commandeered to make their own contribution to the war effort. More importantly there was a sudden exodus of staff as the pace of call-up to the services increased. It was just possible to maintain an adequate complement of teachers, but only through the recruitment of a number of ladies – quite an innovative move for its day. Replacing domestic staff was even harder and with great reluctance it was accepted that it would no longer be possible for the boys to be waited on in the dining hall. A rather undignified self-service arrangement was introduced instead.

Even before the war the School had had its own farm and here the pace and intensity of cultivation were increased. Even so, maintaining the quality of school food was a constant problem, with rabbit appearing on the menu with monotonous regularity. The farm did yield one indirect benefit to Dauntsey's older boys, however, when a large number of land girls was drafted in to help with the work.

During the early part of the war the School's exposure to the realities of conflict was, understandably, negligible, apart from one occasion when during mid-morning break a German bomber flew low over the School, hotly pursued by a Spitfire. The raider was eventually caught and shot down over Salisbury Plain, but it was only later that the School learnt that the Spitfire had actually been piloted by an Old Dauntseian.

By the spring of 1944 it was clear that preparations for a major operation were under way with a significant increase in military activity and convoys trundling through the village at all hours of day and night. So it was with great excitement that the School was gathered together on 6 June to listen to the radio news – almost completely blacked-out for the preceding two months – announcing the invasion of mainland Europe.

Dean Close School, Cheltenham

As with so many other schools, Dean Close suffered from the government's wholesale requisitioning of school buildings at the start of the war. It seems as if the Ministry of Work's strategy during the early months of 1939 was to acquire as many buildings away from London as they could, and worry later about how they were going to use them, or indeed if they were going to use them at all.

Such was Dean Close's fate. An abrupt emptying of the School's buildings was ordered four days after the declaration of war, but in fact the premises lay empty for the following eight months before the School was allowed to return for the summer term 1940.

Plans for a possible evacuation had of course had already been made well in advance, and the senior school set off to share the premises of Monkton Coombe School, some forty miles away. The junior school, with a rather larger proportion of day boys, remained within the town, moving to the premises of Glyngarth prep school.

The enforced cohabitation of Dean Close with Monkton Coombe was not the easiest period in the School's history but with mutual attributes of fortitude and a sense of humour the arrangement was made to work. There was nevertheless a feeling of relief on both sides when it was realised that Dean Close would be allowed to reoccupy its premises in Cheltenham in the spring of 1940.

Once re-established in its own home the School soon became familiar with the constraints and requirements of a country at war. The chapel proved impossible to black out and there are memories of the early communion service on winter Sunday mornings being conducted in subdued candle light as dawn began to filter through the great east window.

In retrospect perhaps the return to Cheltenham in May 1940, spurred by the inactivity of the Phoney War, was premature. By the end of that year German bombs were falling all over England and on 11 December Dean Close was hit. A stick of five high explosive bombs straddled the School's grounds and buildings. The junior school classrooms received a direct hit, and very few panes of glass remained intact in the rest of the buildings. Fortunately most of the School had broken up early for the Christmas holidays, and the only boys still in residence were a group of 12 who had stayed on to sit School Certificate examinations. Everybody present was shocked, but no one was injured, and the boys stoically completed their exams the following day in the library, one of the few rooms still to have windows.

Drama had always been an important element of Dean Close's curriculum and as the war progressed the previously private performances of the Dean Close Players were opened to the public to raise funds for wartime charities. Productions were always carefully chosen, not least John Drinkwater's 'Abraham Lincoln' which was performed in the summer of 1943 when Cheltenham was virtually overrun by American service personnel.

Dover College

One of the few schools that could actually see mainland Europe, Dover College wasted no time in moving from its English Channel location to take up residence with Blundell's School in Tiverton, Devon. The College only remained at Blundell's for one term before moving on to a home of its own at Poltimore House near Exeter.

The return to Dover was made in 1945, and Poltimore House now lies derelict.

Downside School, Purley (now The Lodge School)

The first evacuation of this south London prep school was in the summer of 1939. Some 80 boys and a handful of staff took up residence in the *Barton House Hotel* at Barton-on-Sea in Hampshire. The hotel had initially hoped to continue its traditional business in parallel with housing the School, but its few remaining elderly guests thought otherwise and were quick to make alternative arrangements. The school magazine of the time commented, '… as the last gin and tonic was being served at one end of the cocktail lounge, a blackboard was being set up at the other'.

The hotel garage became an assembly room and gym, the billiard room housed the third form and the sixth form took over the bar.

In the spring of 1940 as the German army occupied France, Downside's location on the south coast became untenable. Boys were withdrawn as parents recognised the emerging dangers, and with only 25 pupils remaining it was decided to return to Purley, with the School reopening in its original premises for the Autumn Term – just as the Blitz started.

The decision to move again was taken only a few weeks after the start of that term. This time the destination was Ogston Hall, a fine country mansion near Higham in Derbyshire. Downside was to merge with another evacuated prep school, Lydgate

House from Norfolk, which had arrived there a couple of terms previously. The debilitating impact of long-distance evacuations was well demonstrated by the fact that the two schools could now only muster 22 pupils between them. This number continued to dwindle to the point at which the combined School was no longer viable, and it eventually closed in December 1943.

Edgar Dodd, the owner and Headmaster of Downside, had in fact resigned from the Ogston Hall school two years previously. He was determined to restart his school in Purley, but the buildings were still occupied by the army. He acquired another property nearby and Downside was reopened in September 1942 – with just two pupils.

The School finally gave up its attempts to dodge German bombs and remained in Purley as V1s rained down on south London during 1944. On the night of 18 June a near miss caused extensive damage to the School's buildings, leaving them unfit for habitation. The occupying soldiers moved out, but it was another six months before a start was made on repairing the bomb damage and clearing up the extensive mess left behind by the military.

The buildings were reopened, somewhat appropriately, on 7 May 1945 – the day of Germany's unconditional surrender. The number of pupils had risen to seventy-six.

Dulwich College Prep School

On 1 September 1939 the School packed up and moved to Cranbrook in Kent. Much of the School took up residence in Coursehorn, a house owned by the Headmaster's in-laws, but some of the younger boys were looked after at Benenden, the well known girls' school also located in Cranbrook.

By June 1940 it became necessary to move further afield, and the long journey was made to Betws-y-coed in north Wales where the *Royal Oak Hotel* became the School's new home. Apparently the Headmaster decided not to tell the pupils' parents about this move until it had been completed, which perhaps accounts for the fact that only four boys were summoned back to England. Had the proposed move been known about in advance it is likely that many more boys would have been withdrawn.

Dulwich College

After two abortive attempts at evacuation the College decided to sit out the war at its own home in the inner London suburbs. As a result its wartime story must be one of the most dramatic of all schools.

The first evacuation took place on 29 September 1938 as war seemed imminent. 400 pupils plus forty staff journeyed in charabancs and cars to a disused fever hospital in the Forest of Dean. The following day Neville Chamberlain returned from Munich declaring that there would be 'peace for our time', and Dulwich, greatly relieved, returned to London after less than a week in exile.

A year later there was no last-minute reprieve from the declaration of war, and this time the College had already prepared a more realistic plan of moving to Tonbridge in Kent where it would share the premises of Tonbridge School. It must have been difficult for the Kentish school and town to accommodate 600 boys from London, which perhaps accounted for the fact that the arrangement only lasted a single term.

By the start of the Spring Term 1940 Dulwich had moved back to its own premises in London. The relative peacefulness of the first half of that year was shattered in July with the start of the Blitz. London was attacked for 91 consecutive days and nights, but with the remarkable imperturbability of the times the *Alleynian* magazine simply commented that 'in spite of this there was a very successful cricket season'.

For many schools fire-watching duties were little more than a theoretical exercise. At Dulwich 19 incendiary bombs fell on the School in the space of two months.

There was damage too from high explosive bombs which were falling all around. The engineering block and several other buildings were hit, and finding a window anywhere on the premises which still contained glass was quite an achievement.

But the British spirit continued to shine through. Surrounded by the chaos of war, one of the College's biggest frustrations was the quantity of bomb shrapnel embedded in the turf of the playing fields which made it necessary to cancel rugby matches.

During the Autumn Term of 1940 London was experiencing seven or eight air–raid warnings each day. Within a couple of weeks the number on the register had dropped from 675 to 450 boys. Parents were desperate to move their families to safer parts of the country. Actual daily attendance at the College dropped to about 350. The missing hundred was made up of those who could not get through the shattered roads and railways to their school in the morning – and those who had not survived the air raids of the previous night.

The end of the Blitz brought a period of comparative calm until the first V1 flying bombs began to descend on London in 1944. In July that year the College suffered a direct hit. Every single room in the School suffered damage in one way or another. Fortunately the bomb exploded at 10 p.m. and no one was injured.

Christopher Gilkes, appointed Master of Dulwich in November 1941, commented thus:

> It was our duty, if we claimed to be a great school, to give a lead to London in resisting the attempts of the enemy to paralyse the normal life of the City, and I am proud to be able to say that we were the only school in London which continued to work above ground, in spite of the dangers and difficulties which beset us.

Dunottar School, Reigate, Surrey

The School remained in Reigate throughout the war. Its buildings fortunately had extensive cellars which were used both as classrooms and dormitories during times of danger.

Ealing Priory School (now St Benedict's School), London

The School had been founded in 1902 by the monks of Downside Abbey as a London teaching establishment. In the 1930s, even before war was declared, it was struggling to survive financially, and the prospect of mass evacuations from London made closure seem almost inevitable. But the Headmaster, Dom Rupert Hall, appealed to the Abbey for on-going support, and he was allowed to continue to run the School for about 50 day boys.

Most of the School's buildings were requisitioned to provide a base for the National Fire Service, and the playground was filled with parked fire engines. Teaching activities were compressed into one large residential building which remained available, and very basic lunches were provided for the boys in the monastic refectory of the Abbey Church.

On 8 October 1940 half of the Abbey Church was destroyed by a delayed action 1,200-pound bomb, and the adjacent building being used by the School suffered shattered windows and collapsed ceilings. A brief closure was inevitable, but it wasn't long before classes were resumed, sometimes several simultaneously, in a single air-raid shelter.

Four years later V1 flying bombs were raining on the capital day and night. The sound of their approaching engines became such a familiar part of the London scene that the boys were only directed to take cover if an engine was actually heard to cut out, at which point the explosion was imminent. The V2 rockets which followed were even more destructive, but fortunately less frequent. Nevertheless, the School had a lucky escape when part of a V2 which had exploded in mid-air fell in the playground during a half-term break.

Ealing Priory was much relieved to survive the war without suffering any casualties, and against the odds managed to achieve a significant increase in pupils during the war years.

Eastbourne College

From September 1939 until June 1940 the south-coast town of Eastbourne continued its peaceful pre-war existence. The only harbinger of the conflict to come was the arrival of a large naval gun sited strategically on the promenade which, on the one occasion it was fired, shattered the windows of nearby hotels.

The College bided its time, but the Headmaster, John Nugee, was quietly making contingency plans for a future evacuation. Eastbourne had always had particularly close relations with Radley College in Abingdon, which now responded very positively and generously to Eastbourne's request for possible temporary accommodation in a safer part of the country.

As France was overrun in the spring of 1940 the time came to go. The staff and boys were only given two days to pack up and organise the move, and on 20 July the College drum and bugle band led the march to the railway station to board a special train to Abingdon.

The first stop was actually at Culham where the junior boys were dropped off to spend a term at Nuneham Park, the home of Lord Harcourt.

At Abingdon the Eastbourne party received a rousing welcome from the boys of Radley, and this friendly and positive attitude characterised the next five years of enforced cohabitation.

This almost instinctive comradeship between the two schools proved to be an essential bond during what turned out to be very testing times. Initially the Eastbourne boys bedded down for the night wherever makeshift space could be found for them – some in the science labs and some in the old gym. Eventually more permanent billets were found in local farms and country houses.

During the summer holidays of 1940, as staff numbers were depleted by the call-up of younger members, it was decided that teaching for both schools would be combined into a single timetable of classes. But even so there were determined efforts to ensure that the separate identities of both schools were preserved. There were Radley versus Eastbourne competitions in most sports, which Radley usually won as the number of Eastbourne's exiled pupils gradually declined. There was, however, one momentous rugby match won against the odds by Eastbourne which is still remembered by the Eastbournians who were there on the day.

Part of the College returned to Eastbourne in September 1942, but it was 1945 before the whole school was fully re-established in its former home. Today plaques at both schools commemorate the five years that they worked and played together.

Edinburgh Academy

Some 400 miles north of London and away from the great industrial centres of England, one might have thought the Academy would have been relatively untouched by the war. But it was not so. The first and most dramatic impact was a veritable stampede of parents withdrawing their boys. Between the Summer and Autumn Terms of 1939 the number of pupils in the upper school virtually halved.

The Academy, entirely dependent on fee income for its continued existence, was thrown into a financial crisis. A drastic reduction in expenditure seemed the only solution. The staff responded with an understanding and commitment that perhaps only a war could inspire. Those who had not already been called up uncomplainingly accepted an immediate 10 per cent cut in their salaries, and took the initiative in researching and recommending other ways in which the school could reduce its costs.

But the financial deficit was still too great, and the Academy eventually had to seek support from Edinburgh Corporation to keep going. The necessary money was forthcoming, but the sums were such that the Corporation wanted to keep a close eye on the way its funds were being used, and as a result the Academy lost its much prized independence. Fortunately, after the nadirs of the early war years, pupil numbers began to recover, driven largely by a dramatic growth in the Academy's prep school from a mere 30 boys in 1939 to nearly 240 in 1945. By that year the Academy had re-established its own financial viability, and it was with much gratitude, but also much relief, that it waved farewell to the Edinburgh Corporation members that had sat on its Board of Directors for the previous five years.

In the early months of the war, with half its pupils gone, much of the Academy was empty. The unused space was rapidly requisitioned by the Edinburgh Auxiliary Fire Service which constructed a 22,000-gallon water tank in the yard and converted some of the classrooms to firemen's quarters.

Inevitably the war changed the priorities of school life – compulsory horticulture frequently replaced compulsory games. Large parts of the school's grounds were turned over to agriculture in one form or another. Sheep grazed on New Field, and the quality of the potato crop became almost as important as the number of boys gaining places at Oxford and Cambridge.

Elizabeth College, Guernsey

Many schools were evacuated during the first year of the war, but not many had to undertake their exodus by sea.

On 22 June 1940 the pupils of Elizabeth College were loaded on to the SS *Batavia IV*, carrying in all nearly 1,000 evacuees from Guernsey, and headed towards the comparative safety of England. A month later the island surrendered to the invading German forces.

The College initially settled in to premises in Oldham where for a fortnight masters struggled to keep exam revision schedules going. Later that summer a new home was found in Great Hucklow in the Peak District, and the senior boys moved into Whitehall, a large country house just north of Buxton. Before additional assistance arrived Mrs Milnes, the Headmaster's wife, single-handedly took on the roles of both cook and matron for some 90 boys.

On Guernsey the College had been mainly a day school, so most of the pupils had to adapt quickly to becoming boarders, and prefects took on extra responsibilities for dormitories and the supervision of meals. Many children had the additional concern of leaving families at home on the island which was now Nazi-occupied territory. Communication was extremely difficult and mainly conducted via the Red Cross.

On top of all this the first winter of the war was a harsh one and the frost and snow of Derbyshire came as a shock to those used to the mild climate of the Channel Islands. The Women's Voluntary Service did stalwart work in rustling up extra warm clothes.

The Channel Islands were liberated on 9 May 1945 and the College returned to its original home a few months later. Its buildings had been well used by the Germans and considerable restoration was required, but normal life was eventually re-established with the start of the Michaelmas Term on 5 October 1945.

Elmhurst School, South Croydon

In the summer of 1939 Elmhurst was confronted with the issue that affected all London schools – to evacuate, or not to evacuate? The natural inclination was to go, but the then Headmaster, Gerald Peachell, was reluctant to abandon Croydon altogether. So Elmhurst decided to do both, and parents were offered the choice of their boys remaining as day pupils in Croydon, or becoming boarders in High Wycombe. The School in effect split into two. Initially the numbers of pupils in the two locations were fairly equal but, as with so many schools that decided to remain in London, the number in Croydon declined rapidly once the war situation became more serious.

Mr Peachell had originally come from High Wycombe and it was in fact his family home, The Cedars, that provided a base for Elmhurst's Buckinghamshire branch. Two nearby semi-detached houses were also purchased and the three buildings between them provided living and teaching accommodation for the staff and boys who were evacuated.

Running the School in two separate locations some fifty miles apart was not easy. In March 1940 the anticipated attacks on England had failed to materialise, and it was announced that the High Wycombe part of the School would definitely return to Croydon for the following September – 'unless the situation makes it impossible'. A prophetic statement. The Battle of Britain and the start of the Blitz did indeed make return impossible, and Elmhurst remained operating in High Wycombe until 1943. As the danger of attack in that year once again seemed to diminish the two parts of the School were reunited in Croydon – just in time for the commencement of the V1 and V2 raids on London.

This time the School decided to stay put. Taking shelter under desks and in the cellars during air raids became almost routine. But although the area around the School suffered considerable bomb damage, Elmhurst itself escaped without a direct hit.

Eltham College, London

As the prospect of war loomed the College, situated in inner London, was mainly concerned with the vulnerability of its boarders. It was decided that the day boys would continue to be taught on site, but all the boarders slept in a single building and a direct hit would have been disastrous.

Taunton School agreed to provide a home for Eltham should the need arise. The fact that both schools had strong connections with the Congregational and Baptist churches provided a common bond. Taunton's generosity was put to the test early when Eltham's boarders were exiled there briefly – on this occasion for just two weeks – at the time of the Munich crisis in 1938.

A year later the boarders travelled once again to Taunton, and this time they were to remain there for six years. In the summer of 1940 they were joined at Taunton by the boys of King's School, Rochester who were also retreating from the dangers of south eastern England.

It was common practice during the war for an evacuated school to share the premises and facilities of its host, but otherwise to remain completely independent of it. Not so at Taunton. It was decided that the three schools would in effect merge and become one. The senior boys of Eltham and Rochester in effect became Tauntonians, albeit temporarily, and in 1942 it was an Eltham pupil who became Head Boy of Taunton. But previous traditional loyalties were not completely forgotten, nor were they discouraged. After a while it was possible to establish separate boarding houses for both Elthamians and Roffensians and this helped to ensure that the evacuated schools' separate identities did not disappear. The old allegiances quickly resurfaced during inter-house competitions. In 1941 Eltham won the rugby cup, and Rochester were house champions at cricket.

Eltham College returned to London in September 1945.

Emanuel School, London

The School left Wandsworth on 1 September 1939. Its own buildings were close to Clapham Junction railway station which was an obvious potential target for enemy bombers.

The boys of Emanuel were taken in by Churcher's College in Petersfield, Hampshire and remained there until 1945, although some tutorial classes were resumed in London as early as the autumn of 1943.

Eothen School, Caterham

Perhaps at the beginning of the war Eothen thought that being nearly 20 miles from the centre of London was sufficient to place it outside the danger zone. The School decided not to evacuate, and subsequently discovered that the Surrey hills were not really a very safe place to be at all.

Pupil numbers dropped dramatically – 'the Autumn Term of 1939 arrived, but the children did not'. The School started that term with only 50 girls, with ages ranging from six to seventeen.

The Headmistress and the relatively few remaining staff prepared for the worst. The swimming pool fund was used to pay for the construction of shelters in the garden, and the appearance of the school buildings was transformed by numerous sandbags, taped up window glass and blackout curtains.

The proximity of the RAF fighter base at Kenley inevitably attracted the attention of the Luftwaffe. High explosive and incendiary bombs fell close by, and local transport was frequently disrupted when roads were closed to allow unexploded bombs to be made safe. The School managed to avoid any serious damage to its buildings, and spirits were lifted as the girls watched the Hurricanes and Spitfires perform victory rolls as they returned to their airfield.

The girls of Eothen were not to be outdone by the local boys' schools when it came to military training. The Girls' Training Corps was formed which marched to gramophone records or the piano and learnt Morse code and semaphore.

The School also opened its doors during the war years to Jewish refugees from mainland Europe and was mightily impressed by the courage, fortitude and determination of those they took in from Poland, Holland, Czechoslovakia and Germany.

Eton College

As one might expect of an educational establishment whose playing fields were supposedly instrumental in the English victory at Waterloo, Eton stood firm in the face of Hitler's menacing ambitions.

The College had occupied its site on the banks of the Thames for five hundred years, and was in no mood to be shifted.

Its bravado was challenged on the night of 4 December 1940 when the College received two direct hits from enemy bombs, but no Etonians were killed or seriously injured.

Farringtons and Stratford House, Chislehurst, Kent

The School received early notification from the authorities that its premises were to be requisitioned for military purposes. But it was not until the end of 1940 that Farringtons actually moved to the *Trecarn Hotel* in Babbacombe, South Devon. Pupil numbers there were much reduced and when the news came that *Trecarn* also was to be commandeered by the RAF, it was decided with great reluctance to close the School.

But there was a determination that this was not to be the end. For five years the spirit of the School was kept alive by the continued production of the school magazine, *The Farringtonian*, which published letters from old girls and staff.

It was not until 1945 that Farringtons was allowed to reoccupy its own buildings. They were in the most appalling condition – filthy dirty and barely a window unbroken. Former members of staff returned and during the early freezing months of 1946 set about the task of restoring the buildings to a useable state.

All their efforts were rewarded on 3 May that year when Farringtons reopened, with 42 pupils and six staff.

Framlingham College, Suffolk

As war broke out Framlingham, a few miles from the East Anglian coast, was worried about its proximity to beaches that could be the target of a German invasion. But the College decided against precipitate moves and waited to see how the war developed. As the autumn of 1939 became winter the usual precautions were taken. Windows were blacked out, gas masks were carried everywhere and fire-watching teams were set up. The College's air-raid shelters were hopelessly inadequate for their purpose, but the official ARP advice to 'scatter the boys in the surrounding countryside' in the event of a raid seemed equally unhelpful.

Less than a year later there was little more than 70 miles of North Sea separating Framlingham from the triumphant might of the German army, and it was time for the College to look for a less vulnerable location. The search for a new home ended when Repton School in Derbyshire offered to share its facilities, and on 6 August 1940 about 100 boarders set off for the midlands. Most of the day boys, who were a minority, remained in Suffolk.

The recollections of the Framlinghamians who were part of their College's brief excursion to Repton exude enthusiasm. Repton's impressive facilities were enjoyed. And, because the two houses occupied by the boys were at opposite ends of Repton, they had the freedom of the town, which they certainly did not have at Framlingham. It was for a time an idyllic summer.

Idyllic for the boys maybe, but not for those who were responsible for them. The intensity of Germany's aggression was increasing. The Blitz had started, and nearby Derby with its manufacturing industry, which included the Rolls Royce aero engine plant, was high on the list of the Luftwaffe's targets. Framlingham had moved from a relatively safe frying pan into a distinctly hot fire.

The Framlingham governors actually decided that the College should return to Suffolk just two weeks after it had been evacuated. Their decision was probably right. The East Anglian beaches were, of course, not invaded, and apart from the occasional stray German bomber and a V1 doodlebug that exploded near the swimming pool in 1944, Framlingham's exposure to enemy action was minimal.

The College reopened for the Autumn Term 1940 back in its own home, perhaps to the disappointment of some of the returning evacuees. Repton had been fun and the bombing of Derby had been exciting. The young seem to have an ability to detach themselves from the fact that bombing is also dangerous and tragic.

In the latter years of the war this excitement for the boys was regenerated to an extent as East Anglia was virtually taken over by the US Air Force. Flying Fortresses and Mustangs roared overhead daily at treetop height, and the occasional crashed aircraft provided the unwittingly callous youngsters with plenty of opportunities for souvenir hunting.

Fulneck Boys' School, Pudsey, Yorkshire

Fulneck Schools, one for boys and one for girls, were founded on the outskirts of Pudsey by the Moravian Church. The two schools amalgamated in 1994.

When the boys returned to their School for the start of the Autumn Term in September 1939 they found it had been transformed during the summer holidays. The staff and Governors had faithfully followed the instructions contained in Government Circular 1467 – 'Air Raid Precautions in Schools'. Trenches, recommended then as the most suitable form of shelter, had been dug in the School grounds, hundreds of sandbags protected the most vulnerable parts of the buildings and every possible source of night-time light had been blacked out. The repeated practices of air-raid procedures in the early uneventful months of the war eventually proved their worth when the sirens started wailing in earnest as the real conflict began.

Although never seriously threatened by enemy action, the School was meticulous in ensuring the safety of its pupils, while at the same time showing a determination to lead life as normally as possible. The traditional service on the last Sunday of the Autumn Term in 1939 was interrupted by the sound of air-raid sirens, and the church emptied in seconds. Undeterred, the service was resumed and completed the following day.

The boys embarked with enthusiasm on a number of schemes to raise money for the war effort, perhaps spurred on by the Fulneck Girls who took the initiative by collecting a significant sum for the Spitfire Fund in early 1941. The School's National Savings group became the focus and driver of these activities and vigorous fundraising enabled contributions to be made to the regular countrywide appeals such as War Ships Week, Wings for Victory and Salute the Soldier.

Classified by the government as being in a 'safe' part of the country, Fulneck immediately began to attract migrants from the danger zones. The number of boys joining the School peaked at 57 in 1943, compared with just six in 1938. Some of these newcomers were refugees escaping from mainland Europe. In the desperate summer months of 1939 children were allowed to leave countries such as Czechoslovakia, but not their parents. So unescorted seven- and eight-year-olds travelled across Europe, the North Sea and England to arrive at Fulneck with no money, few possessions – and not a word of English. In the true tradition of the Moravian Church the School welcomed these strangers into its midst and provided them with a safe haven. New friendships were quickly established, and many of the refugees, some of whom had no news of their families for years, spent the holidays in the homes of their new found Fulneck friends.

Gordonstoun, Elgin, Scotland

Gordonstoun House was requisitioned by the army in 1940 and the School was forced to find alternative accommodation.

Fortunately the father of a boy attending the School owned three houses in Wales, and these became Gordonstoun's temporary home during the war years.

Godolphin and Latymer School, Hammersmith, London

The School's search for a home away from London in 1939 ended when Newbury County School offered to share its premises.

The whole School made the move out of town at the start of the war, but as early as 1940 some staff and children had moved back to London, and by 1943 the return had been completed.

Gresham's School, Holt, Norfolk

The wartime Headmaster of Gresham's had a fondness for Cornwall, particularly the county's Atlantic coast. So in 1940, when Norfolk was deemed to be too close to Germany for comfort, the School headed to Newquay.

And there it remained until 1944 when it returned home across the country, proudly bearing an inscribed silver cup presented by Newquay's Local Defence Volunteers to the School's Officer Training Corps for its very effective patrolling of the coastline.

Haileybury, Hertford

During the long hot summer holidays of 1939 the staff and senior boys at Haileybury prepared for war. Air-raid shelters were dug, fire-watching parties organised and over 3,000 windows painted black.

Everyone waited – but during the Autumn Term of that year the lack of expected military activity was almost an anticlimax. A bad outbreak of chicken-pox seemed more serious than the war. The editor of *The Haileyburian* commented '… That gentleman [Hitler] has really disturbed Haileybury remarkably little.'

It was rumoured that the whole School was to be requisitioned by the Ministry of Health to provide a huge hospital for the people of East Anglia. But the School had influential friends in high places. A discreet appeal to Old Haileyburian Clement Attlee, who was a member of the War Cabinet and subsequently Churchill's Deputy Prime Minister, successfully removed the main threat to the School and only one block was taken over.

Eventually the war came to Haileybury. The School was close enough to London to be in the midst of intense bombing during the Blitz. At least 26 bombs exploded around the School, but shattered windows were the worst damage it experienced.

At the time of Dunkirk several senior boys from nautical families were 'absent' for a number of days. No questions were asked.

It was rumoured that Lord Haw Haw, the German propagandist, expressed the hope that Haileybury would not be hit as he wanted to send his son there after the war. A further rumour was that German bomb aimers were instructed to avoid hitting the school quadrangle as its paths provided a useful landmark from the air.

By January 1941 the number of pupils attending Haileybury had fallen to 374 and the School was struggling financially. The Imperial Service College at Windsor, with which Haileybury had previous connections, was suffering similarly and it was decided that the two establishments would combine on Haileybury's site. The merger took place in the summer of 1942 and returned the number at the School to over 500 pupils.

Many boys joined the armed forces as soon as they left school. Some who qualified as pilots with the RAF were in the habit of demonstrating their new-found skills to those who remained at the School, which caused the editor of *The Haileyburian and ISC Chronicle* to comment ... 'May I appeal to those OH aviators who with deadly accuracy miss the top of Chapel dome by an inch or two to choose some other way to salute the Old School and to employ the government's petroleum for more immediate purposes.'

By 1942 the threat of a German invasion had all but disappeared and wartime life at the School became less tense. But it was not long before London was once again under attack from V1s and V2s. Hertford town was hit, yet all the School's buildings survived intact, with only minor damage.

The announcement of Germany's unconditional surrender on 7 May 1945 was greeted with an outburst of exuberance and excitement which the prefects controlled with difficulty. The following day, VE Day, was declared a holiday which ended with a party around an immense bonfire, with the massed searchlights of London painting the night sky in the distance.

Harrow School

Before the start of the war Harrow was declared by the government to be a 'neutral' area, which meant that evacuation was not compulsory. As the Blitz intensified in the autumn of 1940 the School's decision not to move perhaps in retrospect seemed a trifle relaxed. A number of fires were caused by incendiary bombs, most of which were extinguished by the School's own fire-fighting parties.

The buildings escaped major damage from high explosive bombs, several of which fell in the grounds, with one most annoyingly creating a large crater in the recently levelled 1st XV rugby pitch.

Everything was in short supply. To save fuel boys could only have fires in their rooms on alternate evenings, and they took it in turns to share the warm rooms with their neighbours. During daytime fires were only allowed in the main communal rooms.

With all boys confined to their houses during the hours of darkness, keeping them entertained was a problem. Films were sometimes shown, but home-made entertainment also became popular and concert parties, consisting of musical items and sketches and involving both masters and boys, were regular events.

Morale was raised in December 1940 when the School was visited by perhaps the most important Old Harrovian of the time, Winston Churchill, along with several other Old Harrovian members of the government. A musical programme had been arranged which ended with the Prime Minister joining in enthusiastically with school songs, many of which he sang from memory. Churchill Songs became an annual event at the end of which the Prime Minister would retire to the Headmaster's drawing room, relax with a whisky and cigar and answer questions from the monitors.

The event that probably had the greatest impact on Harrow during the war occurred in the spring of 1942 when the School was asked to accommodate the staff and pupils of Malvern College. The College had been evacuated to Blenheim Palace at the start of the war, but this temporary home was now also to be requisitioned, and Malvern was given three weeks to find alternative premises. Harrow's own pupil numbers had dropped significantly since the start of the war so there were few difficulties in finding space to accommodate Malvern, but the prospect of the sharing arrangement raised many doubts and concerns over whether the two schools would be able to retain their separate identities. In the event the problems were minimal. The Malvern boys were assigned to boarding houses of their own and teaching facilities were shared in a spirit of friendly co-operation. Both schools maintained their own customs and uniforms alongside one another until Malvern was able to return to its original home in Worcestershire in 1946. An apocryphal tale was told of one family who, having registered their son for Harrow before the war, decided at the last minute to switch him to Malvern 'where he would be safer'. What they subsequently thought about their Malvernian son being relocated to wartime Harrow is not recorded.

Highgate School, London

The Senior School evacuated to Westward Ho! in 1939. The Junior School initially went to Hartland Abbey, but subsequently joined up with the seniors at Westward in 1941.

Hull High School

The School moved from its location in the centre of Hull to Heversham in Cumberland at the southern end of the Lake District, where the girls were accommodated in four houses.

The School never returned to Hull. At the end of the war in 1945 it set up in new premises at Tranby Croft in the East Riding of Yorkshire, but still retained its original name.

Today, after over sixty years, the four houses of Hull High School still bear the names of the Heversham properties used during the war.

Hulme Grammar School, Oldham

It was June 1940 before the lives of those at Hulme were seriously affected by the war. Up to then there had been air-raid practices and the compulsory carrying of gas masks in their brown cardboard cases, but little else to disrupt the routine of school life.

All this changed in the summer of 1940 when the Headmaster, Mr Shaw, volunteered to take in evacuees from the Channel Islands. With the German invasion imminent, rapid arrangements were made for the boys of the Guernsey State Intermediate School to leave the island. On 22 June they were loaded into the hold of a cattle ship and set off across the Channel, trying to avoid the attentions of German aircraft.

Although Oldham presented them with a totally different environment from that which they had known at home, The Guernsey Boys, as they became known, took to their new surroundings with enthusiasm. A proposal that some of them should move to Elizabeth College in Buxton was met with such a lack of interest that it was never implemented.

It was decided that the two schools would retain their separate identities and remain independent of one another as far as teaching was concerned. Guernsey in effect became a school within a school. But the allocation of classrooms seemed to be somewhat random, and there were times when groups of Guernsey boys were led around the buildings by a master seeking an unoccupied room in which the lesson could be started.

The pupils of both schools came together for morning prayers and assemblies, which were taken in turn by the two Headmasters. These two gentlemen were apparently of very different character and temperament. Mr Fulford, the Headmaster of Guernsey Intermediate, was described as being ' a rather flamboyant man who had a marvellous sense of humour', while Mr Shaw was much more formal in his approach. The relationship between the two was understandably a little edgy at times.

But differences were not allowed to disrupt the otherwise harmonious co-existence of the two establishments, and Hulme continued to provide a haven for the Guernsey school until it returned to its island home in 1945.

Hurstpierpoint College, Sussex

As war broke out the College no doubt felt reasonably safe in its Sussex location well away from London. The fact that the south coast, on which invading German forces could easily have landed, was only ten miles to the south did not deter the College from its decision not to move.

As with so many other schools that did not have to suffer the rigours of their own evacuations, Hurstpierpoint was generous in making its facilities available to other schools that did feel the need to move away from locations in or close to London.

Firstly Westminster School asked the College in the summer of 1939 to take in boarders from two of its houses – 90 boys in all, of whom 42 were found accommodation within the College itself, with the remaining 48 being billeted in the village. The arrangements for the Westminster boys to continue their education at Hurstpierpoint did not work particularly well, and were discontinued after only two terms.

But after less than a year, in January 1941, Hustpierpoint was again asked to play host, this time to Downsend, a prep school from Leatherhead. The Downsend boys remained until March 1942 when it was deemed safe for them to return to Surrey, but some had become so integrated into Hurstpierpoint that they decided to remain and were absorbed into its Junior House.

In 1942 the well-being of the School was threatened, not by enemy action, but by the Air Ministry which apparently wished to requisition its buildings and grounds to construct an airfield. Their proposal would have involved the demolition of several school buildings and probably the chapel tower, as well as the removal of all the trees. A vociferous protest was made and there was much relief when it was discovered that the whole scheme had resulted from a mistake made by a Ministry official.

It gradually became clear that Hurstpierpoint's decision to remain in Sussex during the war was a sound one. Over six years pupil numbers rose from 159 to 260 and the School grew in strength both financially and academically.

Hurst View School, South Croydon

Hurst View was a co-educational prep school which soldiered on even after its first building was burnt to the ground by an incendiary bomb.

An alternative home for the School was found which fortunately had large cellars where lessons could continue during air raids.

Hymers College, Hull

Hull was considered to be a possible target for German bombers and the decision was taken in 1939 to retreat to the Yorkshire countryside. It was not possible to find a new temporary home for the complete School, so the seniors went to Pocklington School, whose facilities they shared, and the juniors went to Market Weighton.

Neither of these two locations was more than twenty miles away from Hull, but both were in the country and away from the coast.

Hymers returned to Hull in September 1943.

Ibstock Place (previously the Froebel School), Roehampton

Before the war the Froebel School had premises in West Kensington from which they departed in September 1939, and which subsequently suffered serious bomb damage. The School moved to Freeland near Oxford, where it only stayed for a few months before moving on again to Little Gaddesden in Hertfordshire.

The return to London was made possible at the end of the war when new premises in Ibstock Place, Roehampton were purchased in August 1945. It took more than a year to remove the building's wartime occupants – the Ministry of Works and Planning, and also the Army Ordnance Research Group – and restore it for school use. But eventually in October 1946 the School reopened in its new home, having adopted a new name to reflect its new location.

The John Lyon School, Harrow

The School did not evacuate, nor did it host any other school, but its senior pupils made their contribution to the war effort by working on farms in the countryside to the west of London. After D-Day they helped to maintain the massive flow of supplies sent across the Channel to the invading forces by helping out at the Royal Army Ordnance Corps depot at Northolt.

Kelly College, Tavistock

The College hosted Arundel House School for a year at the start of the war.

Kent College, Canterbury

Evacuation took place in June 1940 when the College's buildings were requisitioned by the RAF. The day boys went nearby to Simon Langton Grammar School, which itself only remained in Canterbury for a further three months before moving to Wantage.

The boarders – about 80 of them – went further afield to join up with Truro School in Cornwall, which like Kent College had a strong Methodist ethos. Although the arrival of the College contingent stretched Truro's accommodation and facilities it was a saving grace in one respect. Both schools had suffered an almost instant loss of younger members of staff to the armed forces. Truro's Headmaster said that without the arrival of the admittedly depleted Kent College staff he would have had difficulty continuing to run his own school.

Although initially some College boys had to sleep in Truro's gymnasium, the majority were accommodated in *Tremorvah House*, a local hotel, and eventually *Tremorvah* together with one or two other houses nearby became Kent College's home base in Cornwall.

The two schools retained their separate identities, but combined for academic purposes thus making the best use of the scarce teaching resources. Games facilities were shared and the boys from Kent were soon influenced by the local Cornish enthusiasm for rugby, which quickly displaced soccer as a primary winter sport.

Kent College's wartime Headmaster, John Prickett, was determined that the School would return to Canterbury as soon as it was possible to do so. Indeed, he frequently travelled to Kent to promote the School in its home town. His efforts proved successful, not least because he offered to look after his pupils in Cornwall during the holidays as well as term time. As the intensity of war increased more and more parents were happy to move their children away from the worst scenes of action and, although pupil numbers initially dropped a little after the evacuation, Kent College eventually returned to Canterbury in 1945 with more boys than it had taken away five years previously. This was a particularly impressive achievement when one considers that a large proportion of the original college evacuees attained school-leaving age during the years at Truro. In fact the number of boys who were at the College in Canterbury at both the beginning and end of the war was less than twenty.

Most of the boys revelled in the more relaxed rural environment of the West Country, but not so all the staff. One senior member of the common room recorded his impressions of Cornwall thus … 'It is remote and exceedingly primitive. Civilisation in many of its aspects has not yet penetrated this benighted county. It is a crude and unlovely spot.'

But there can be no doubting the deep gratitude that the Headmaster and staff of Kent College felt and frequently expressed to Truro School for its unfailing hospitality and friendship in troubled times.

Kent College for Girls, Pembury

Before the war the College for Girls was in Folkestone – from where mainland Europe can be viewed on a good day. The increasingly firm belief that war was about to be declared in September 1938 was sufficient to persuade the Governors to evacuate the School at very short notice. Indeed the pupils had less than 24 hours to prepare for their departure to Penzance in Cornwall.

On 28 September the Headmistress, staff and 82 girls travelled to the West Country. The plan was to take over the old premises of the West Cornwall School, which had recently moved into a new building, but for two nights the girls were billeted in homes around the town while they waited for their bedding and possessions to arrive.

West Cornwall School's old premises turned out to be seriously old. The only lighting was sparsely distributed gas lamps and on the first and only night it was occupied there seemed to be more rain inside the building than there was outside. The girls were transferred to a local hotel the following day.

Two days after the College arrived in Penzance Neville Chamberlain flew back from Munich to announce that there would be no war. The decision was taken to return, without undue haste, to Folkestone. Plans to set up some form of basic teaching timetable were virtually abandoned and the children enjoyed a pleasant opportunity to explore the sights of Cornwall.

On 7 October the College returned to Folkestone. But it was not to remain there long. A move away from the coast had been considered as early as 1937, and in the summer of 1939 contracts were signed to acquire Hawkwell Place at Pembury. The College opened there at the start of the following Autumn Term.

Any thoughts that the new location would be a safer one were of course ill-founded. In 1940 the Battle of Britain raged overhead and the surrounding Kentish countryside became known as 'bomb alley'. A Hurricane fighter crashed in the College grounds and the constant danger was brought into sharper focus when an enemy fighter pilot was arrested as he hung suspended in his parachute in a nearby tree. The girls cycled the country lanes expecting to be confronted by an invasion force at any moment.

The abundant presence in the area of young soldiers of varying nationalities did provide a degree of distraction for the older girls, and excitement reached a peak when the College was 'captured and occupied' during an exercise involving Canadian troops.

There was almost hysterical jubilation on the night of 7 May 1945 when the cessation of hostilities was announced on the 10 o'clock news. The younger girls were woken in their dormitories to join in the instant celebration, and indulged in a mass hurling of gas masks out of the windows on to the lawns below.

Kimbolton School, Huntingdon

Kimbolton remained in its own home throughout the war. Its closest connection with military activities came from the use of a nearby airfield by American bombers between 1943 and 1945. Some at the School became friendly with the Americans at the base and enduring friendships were established.

King Edward's School, Birmingham

In September 1939 the decision to move away from the Birmingham area was made for the School by the local evacuation officer who decreed that its new home would be Repton in Derbyshire where Repton School had offered to provide accommodation and facilities. Old Mitre, previously one of Repton's boarding houses, was made available as a teaching block for the King Edward's boys. It was an attractive ivy-covered building from the outside, but the interior was in a relatively advanced state of decay. The only form of heating was tiny fireplaces, which never seemed to get used.

The boys were allocated to billets around the village, and seemed to be moved from one to another at fairly frequent intervals. The local countryside plus the nearby towns of Burton and Derby provided the Edwardians with new opportunities for exploration, which for seniors included the building of liaisons with the local population of young females. This practice became known as 'sparking'. It was severely frowned upon by the School staff, including the Headmaster, but it is doubtful whether such disapproval proved to be much of an inhibitor for the boys.

When war broke out King Edward's had been in the process of building an entirely new school complex at Birmingham. Work on this had been allowed to continue during the months of the Phoney War and by the summer of 1940 the new premises were almost complete. So the decision was taken to depart from Repton and return home.

'Almost complete' turned out to be a bit of an exaggeration and considerable compromise and ingenuity was required to extract the maximum usage from those buildings that had been finished. One of these was the dining hall, but the splendid new surroundings could not compensate for the rapid decline in the quantity and quality of wartime school meals. Sixth formers, who were allowed to leave the school premises at lunchtimes, headed enthusiastically to the local British Restaurant – part of a chain sponsored by the government during the war to provide cheap and nutritious food for the general public – where a main course and pudding of better quality than the School's could be purchased for sixpence (2.5p).

In spite of Birmingham suffering numerous air raids, the School's new buildings remained virtually unscathed. The city's tram system was frequently disrupted by the previous night's bombing, however, which meant that some boys had long walks to school in the morning, collecting souvenirs of shrapnel lying about the streets as they went.

King Edward VI Camp Hill School, Birmingham

The whole School departed for Warwick on 1 September 1939. The town is not too far distant from Birmingham and yet its lack of industry made it unlikely to attract the attentions of the German bombers. Camp Hill had been offered and accepted the use of Warwick School's facilities during the afternoons.

On arrival in Warwick the evacuees were allocated to billets, some in Warwick Castle itself, and the Camp Hill boys waited apprehensively for the war to begin, anticipating a sky black with enemy aircraft. Of course it didn't happen – or at least not for a while. Autumn gave way to a bitterly cold winter and still there was no serious conflict, apart from some intense snowball battles between the boys of Warwick and Camp Hill.

By the early spring of 1940 boys had begun to drift back to Birmingham, and this gradual migration persuaded the Camp Hill authorities that the School itself should return home. It reopened in its own premises in September – just in time for the first serious bombing raids to hit the city.

By November the position was becoming untenable. The School itself had suffered some damage and the announcement was made that Camp Hill was to embark on its second evacuation, this time to Lichfield.

Disembarking from the train at Lichfield station the party was directed to the Congregational Hall where the plan was to match evacuees with local families who had agreed to host. Unfortunately there were more evacuees than there were hosts, and in desperation a temporary arrangement was made to house the leftover group of six boys at the home of the Lord Bishop of Lichfield. The Bishop lived in a splendid 17th-century palace which must have been one of the most exceptional and impressive billets enjoyed by any schoolboy throughout the whole war.

The unexpected arrival of six 11- to 13-year-olds must have caused a degree of disruption to the previously well ordered ecclesiastical life of the Palace. But the Bishop's wife grew fond of the boys and the temporary billet became permanent.

Only occasionally did the Bishop run out of goodwill and patience. But when an impromptu game of football in the Palace courtyard resulted in a broken pane of stained glass in a chapel window he was moved to write to the boys' parents expressing his wish that they should take immediate steps to '.... inculcate in your boy some sense of discipline and of obedience'.

Camp Hill remained in Lichfield for two years. Classes were held in the Congregational Hall, and later on at the local grammar school as well. But by 1942, as the threat of air attack diminished, boys once again started to return to Birmingham, and later that year Camp Hill opened its doors once more in its old home.

King Edward VI Five Ways School, Birmingham

The School's evacuation to Monmouth had been well planned during the spring and summer of 1939. But, as the political situation in Europe rapidly deteriorated in the closing days of August, the order to move was given at short notice. Many of the staff and pupils of Five Ways were still scattered in summer holiday locations. One master was in Cornwall when he received the call to return. He drove back overnight, arriving at the School at eight in the morning, and was promptly assigned the task of organising the evacuation.

On 1 September 350 boys, 20 masters and ten lady helpers marched in a long column to Snow Hill station and boarded the train for Monmouth. The authorities of the Welsh town, and indeed the residents who had offered to provide billets for the pupils, had been expecting a girls' school. But after some rapidly changed arrangements the town adjusted well to the unanticipated influx of young men.

At the start, boys, masters and lady helpers were scattered around billets in the town, surrounding hamlets and even isolated farmhouses. Not an ideal arrangement, and eventually it was decided to buy several of the large properties that lay empty in the town and convert them into boarding houses. By October 1941 the School had seven such hostels in use which between them housed 130 boys.

Educational life quickly settled into a pattern with Monmouth School's buildings being used for class work during the afternoons. A wide range of extra-curricular activities was also soon under way using a variety of premises across the town.

Parental visits were organised on two or three Sundays each term with coaches laid on to transport the mothers and fathers between Birmingham and Monmouth. And as life in Birmingham became more dangerous, parents were increasingly keen for Five Ways boys to remain at Monmouth during the holidays. The group of 30 that spent Christmas there in 1939 grew to 100 the following year. Holiday activities for the boys were improvised with great creativity by the staff, many of whom worked without any sort of a break for over a year.

There is no doubt that Five Ways' evacuation to Monmouth was a success even though it did not embrace the whole School. In September 1939 the parents of some 120 boys chose for them to remain in Birmingham. Many of these initially participated in a study scheme which involved attending school once or twice a week and working on assignments at home. In the following year 40 Five Ways boys attended classes at Kings Norton Grammar School which was in a less vulnerable area.

By February 1944 the drift back to Birmingham from Monmouth had reduced the number of boys in Wales to less than 200, and the Governors decided that the evacuation was to come to an end. During the summer holidays that year the School packed its belongings, emptied the buildings it had occupied and said a final farewell to the Welsh town which had provided it with a happy home for five years.

King Edward VI School, Southampton

The School was destined to spend the war years sharing the premises of Poole Grammar School, some 30 miles along the coast. In the summer of 1939 parents of day boys were faced with tough decisions as to whether their children should leave home and be billeted with strangers, or whether they should remain in the high-risk environs of Southampton. King Edward's started the Autumn Term in Poole with just under two-thirds of the previous term's pupils.

The evacuation took place on 2 September and boys were assigned to billets all over Poole. Goodwill and enthusiasm were perhaps more in evidence than organisational skill because it took the Headmaster a further two days to track down where all his boys had gone.

The sharing of Poole Grammar School's facilities worked relatively smoothly but King Edward's felt the need also for a place of its own to help preserve the School's separate identity. Eventually Ledgard House in Poole was rented and converted into a little home away from home, furnished with many pictures and library books brought across from Southampton.

The decision to evacuate proved to be a wise one. The School's new buildings in Southampton, which had only been completed in 1938 and then requisitioned by the army at the start of the war, suffered bomb damage in both 1940 and 1942.

While at Poole the boys took on a number of tasks that contributed to the war effort, not least organising the gathering of scrap metal. By June 1940 they were credited with having collected ten tons, including an abandoned car and motor cycle.

Compared with pre-war days the School's activities at Poole were inevitably restricted but life nevertheless settled into a pattern. Examinations continued to be passed, and there was a steady flow of awards, university places and scholarships for the senior boys. But by 1944, as the danger to England subsided, there was an increasing yen to return home to Southampton. The Governors lacked enthusiasm for this idea so the Headmaster decided that an unusual demonstration might make his point. He and six prefects organised a march on a November morning from Christchurch to Southampton to present a petition to the Chairman, Sir Sidney Kimber. The gesture was dismissed as ridiculous, but perhaps it achieved its purpose. Pressure was brought to bear on the War Office to relinquish the School's buildings, which it eventually did in the spring of 1945, and King Edward's triumphantly reopened for the Summer Term back in Southampton.

In 1999, the 60th anniversary of the evacuation, 40 Old Edwardian evacuees gathered again for a reunion in Poole to commemorate their School's six years of exile.

Kings Monkton School, Cardiff

The only adverse effect of the war was the loss of the School's sports ground. A search was made for an alternative facility and as a result of some useful local connections the School was offered use of no less a venue than Cardiff Arms Park, the famous international rugby ground. The boys took great delight in running out on to the hallowed turf every Wednesday afternoon.

King's School, Rochester

The School's first move, in September 1939, was relatively local – just to the Weald of Kent. The following year, as the prospect of a German invasion of England became more real, it was decided to move away from the south east altogether, and arrangements were made for King's to be hosted by Taunton School in Somerset. The second move, which took place in June 1940, was timely because later that summer the skies over the Weald of Kent became the main arena in which the Battle of Britain was fought out.

King's remained at Taunton for the rest of the war and were joined there by Eltham College from south London.

King's School, Worcester

The School evacuated to Criccieth in Wales in September 1939 but returned to Worcester in April of the following year.

Kingswood School, Bath

Kingswood's buildings were taken over by the Admiralty in 1939 and from then until 1946 the School was hosted by Uppingham in the quiet countryside of Rutland.

The evacuation took place during the summer holidays of 1939. Staff and senior boys were drafted in to help with the exercise and no fewer than 27 railway wagons were needed to transport everything that had to be moved. To start with, the boys' billets were spread across 14 different buildings in the town. These were mainly Uppingham boarding houses, but two small licensed hotels were also used in which some of the older boys undoubtedly and probably illegally experienced their first taste of alcohol.

The two schools were very different from one another. Kingswood was a Methodist establishment with many of its pupils coming from church families, while Uppingham was one of England's top public schools attended by the sons of some of the country's leading families. The Kingswood boys could not help but be impressed by the number of Rolls Royces that arrived on the day of Uppingham's prize-giving. Uppingham's ethos was formal, strict and hierarchical, with fagging still a key component of school society. Kingswood's style was rather more relaxed. The black jackets, pinstripe trousers and boaters of the students from the senior public school contrasted dramatically with the tweed uniforms and caps of the lads from Bath.

The arrival of Kingswood must undoubtedly have disrupted the disciplined routine of Uppingham, but the host school shared its facilities with the newcomers without complaint even to the extent of handing over its gymnasium building completely to provide a dining hall for its guests.

Although the two schools were thrown together into a combined life they both continued to preserve their independent identities. There was no animosity between them, but little communication either. Several Kingswood old boys of the time recall seeing the Uppingham students every day, but rarely speaking to any of them.

Much credit is given to the Headmasters of the two schools who worked extremely well together and jointly managed a successful cohabitation which had the potential to generate many more problems than actually occurred. They decided together that it was probably better if the two schools did not compete with one another at games, recognising that over enthusiastic rivalry on the sports' field could develop into more serious conflicts that would disrupt the delicate balance of harmony they worked so hard to achieve.

Kingswood's evacuation to Uppingham lasted almost seven years before the School eventually returned to Bath in 1946. There is therefore a group of Kingswood old boys who never attended their school in its own home. Their public school years were all spent at Uppingham.

After over half a century there is still a strong bond between the two schools, and in 1996 a dinner was held to commemorate the end of what is still frequently referred to as the 'fortunate exile'.

Lancing College, Sussex

As England anticipated the imminent outbreak of war in 1938 at the time of Munich, the south coast was considered to be a vastly safer location than central London. The Lancing Headmaster, Frank Doherty, offered refuge to Westminster School, where he had himself been a pupil. The Westminster boys only remained briefly at Lancing on that occasion, but returned in September 1939 when war became a reality.

By the summer of 1940 the sounds of the battle in France could be heard on the Sussex downs, and hospital ships began arriving in Shoreham harbour. Realising that the nearby Channel beaches could soon be the landing ground of an invading German army, Lancing decided it was time to move. Apparently little prior thought had been given to the possibility of an evacuation, but at very short notice Ellesmere College in Shropshire agreed to take in three Lancing houses, and the remainder was offered accommodation by Denstone College in Staffordshire. The Westminster contingent departed for a new home at Exeter University.

The army moved swiftly to requisition Lancing's emptying buildings, and within days they had become the headquarters of General Montgomery's 3rd Division. Winston Churchill visited the College a few days after the military had moved in.

Life at Ellesmere and Denstone was brief and chaotic. The arrival of Lancing seriously stretched the facilities at both locations. The hunt for a more permanent home resulted in the acquisition of four separate country houses around Ludlow – Moor Park, which became the College's main base, and Stokesay Court, Ashford Court and Caynham Court which were used as boarding houses. With several miles of Shropshire countryside separating the four locations this was not the easiest way to run the College, but with a degree of goodwill and compromise from all concerned the arrangement was made to work. The whole School would congregate at Moor Park in the mornings, where night-time dormitories were swiftly converted into daytime classrooms. Lessons ended at midday when the boys from the outlying houses would return to their bases for private study during the afternoons.

Back in Lancing the College's requisitioned buildings were soon transferred from the army to the navy and became a training school for new naval officers, with the title HMS *King Alfred*. This apparently caused some confusion for the Nazi propaganda machine as one of Lord Haw Haw's evening broadcasts proudly announced that HMS *King Alfred* had been sunk – an early example of publicity 'spin' stretching credibility too far.

The College eventually returned to Sussex in the spring of 1945. The armed forces had left the buildings and grounds in need of much refurbishment, and the task of packing up and moving all the College's possessions from four different locations in Shropshire was monumental. For long-serving staff the return was filled with nostalgia and emotion. Not so for the boys. Almost without exception the pupils of 1945 had joined the College after its evacuation, and the return for them was not so much a homecoming as the start of a whole new era in their schooldays.

Leamington High School (now known as The Kingsley School)

As evacuation plans were prepared Leamington Spa was considered to be a relatively safe area, but nearby Coventry was deemed to be a danger zone – a judgement that was to be proved horrendously correct just a year later.

At the start of the war the High School hosted 170 girls from two Coventry schools, Barr's Hill and Stoke Park, but by the summer of 1940 it was decided that both schools should return to their own premises. It could not have been a worse decision.

On the night of 14 December 1940 Coventry was subjected to the most concentrated bombing attack that any city suffered throughout the whole war. The city was virtually destroyed.

The High School did its best to alleviate the distress and concern of Coventry's citizens. Several girls who lived close to Coventry were evacuated into the homes of fellow pupils who lived in Leamington.

Leighton Park School, Reading

The declaration of war raised some issues for Leighton Park which were different from most other schools. Its Quaker origins and ethos, and its consequent commitment to pacifism and conscientious objection, posed difficult questions for younger staff and senior boys for whom conscription was likely in the future. Religious conviction may have barred some of them from participating in the conflict itself, but the determination to support their country's war effort in other ways was undiminished. At least one member of staff and a number of Old Leightonians solved their problems of conscience by joining the Friends' Ambulance Unit which did sterling work throughout the war.

Reading, although only 35 miles away from London, was classified as a Reception Area for evacuees, which provided the School with more opportunities to help those most directly affected by the conflict. Many of the evacuees came from the East End of London, and the School's Grove House was made available as a home for pregnant mothers. This same house was subsequently requisitioned by the RAF and used as accommodation for members of the Women's Auxiliary Air Force – a turn of events which proved popular with some of Leighton Park's more senior boys.

All pupils were encouraged to make their own contributions to the war effort. Help was provided to local farmers, and acres of the school grounds were dug up to cultivate potatoes and other vegetables.

Sixth formers took it on themselves to help out at local primary and nursery schools whose young male teachers had already been drafted into the armed services. Regular visits were made to coach soccer, cricket and gymnastics.

The Bursar turned his hand to pig farming, which certainly helped to augment the School's meagre ration of pork and bacon, and the scout troop was always on hand with its trek carts to help evacuees move their possessions to new homes.

In many ways the character of Leighton Park was developed and strengthened by the war years, and in one of the ironies of the time, the pacifist Headmaster, Mr E.B. Castle, was heard to declare that his Quaker school was in fact in better shape at the end of the conflict than it was at the beginning.

The Leys School, Cambridge

Life in Cambridge remained relatively untouched by the early months of the war, with just a few evacuated schoolchildren from London to be accommodated.

The much more threatening circumstances of 1940 developed with startling rapidity.

Hitler's propaganda machine announced that, because of the large number of RAF personnel training in the area, Cambridge had been classified as a primary target for the German bombers. Almost simultaneously The Leys was advised that its buildings would almost certainly be requisitioned to provide an extension to Addenbrooke's Hospital.

Evacuation was inevitable. Various possible new homes for the School were considered, including Gleneagles, but eventually the *Atholl Palace Hotel* in Pitlochry was selected. The hotel had hosted the refined young ladies of Queen Margaret's School during the First World War. The boys of The Leys proved to be rather different guests.

The hotel was capable of accommodating 208 people and was luxuriously fitted with 42 bathrooms and central heating throughout. During the summer holidays of 1940 an advance party toiled to convert the hotel into a school. Lounges were transformed into classrooms, the ballroom became the assembly hall, the solarium housed the chemistry and physics labs – and the nine-hole golf course was 'restructured' to provide three rugby pitches.

Tales from most evacuated schools are filled with descriptions of the ever declining quantity and quality of wartime food. The Leys fared better than most in this respect. In the heart of the Scottish countryside it was not uncommon for venison and salmon to appear on the menu, and sometimes even crayfish as well. Although some of these exotic meals were sourced quite legally, there was no doubt that some of the food was procured by more nefarious methods. In short, some Leysians became more than competent poachers. A historical booklet published by the *Atholl Palace Hotel* reports, 'Not all the local landowners were happy. This arose from an unfortunate misunderstanding over the ownership of their trout, salmon, hares, pheasants, rabbits – indeed, anything edible or saleable.' Some Pitlochry rabbit even found its way by train as far south as Cambridge where it was gratefully received by the parents of several Leysian boys.

The mountainous Scottish countryside – such a contrast to the flatlands around Cambridge – provided enormous excitement and enjoyment to the evacuees, but it also presented perils to the inexperienced. Tragedy struck in March 1941 when two boys on a scouting exercise fell into a deep gorge and were killed. A member of the School staff also died in an accident at the Tummell Falls in September 1944.

In 1943 as the war progressed to an increasingly inevitable victory, The Leys' Governors sensed that Addenbrooke's Hospital would not easily relinquish their hold on the School's Cambridge buildings, which by then housed 400 beds. Indeed it took two years of argument and negotiation before the Minister of Health finally agreed to vacate the buildings in November 1945. During that December working parties restored the *Atholl Palace* to something resembling a hotel, and the Addenbrooke's Hospital extension once more became The Leys School, which reopened in its old home in January 1946.

The Limes Preparatory School, South Croydon

The Limes evacuated to Dane Hill in Sussex in 1939, and its premises in South Croydon were taken over by the army.

In 1946, shortly after its return to Croydon, The Limes became the preparatory department of Croham Hurst School.

Lord Wandsworth College, Hook, Hampshire

The College felt no need to move from its relatively rural location, even though it was thought that the nearby RAF station at Odiham might attract the attention of German aircraft. In the event the airfield was largely untouched by enemy action. The reason it seems was that the base had actually been opened in 1937 by a marshal of the Luftwaffe. He had been so impressed by what he had seen that he had earmarked it for use as his headquarters once England had been invaded, and gave his pilots strict instructions not to drop bombs on it.

Although Odiham was spared it was not unusual to see aerial combat in progress in the skies above the College, and on one occasion an English aircraft crash-landed in the grounds close to the junior house. When the authorities eventually arrived to remove the wreck they found it in rather worse condition than when it had come down. The boys had got there first and gathered an impressive array of souvenirs.

The College was fortunate in being set within 1,300 acres of farm land, and a great variety of produce from this helped to alleviate the rigours of rationing. The boys nevertheless sometimes had to cope with idiosyncrasies in their diet. On one occasion the Bursar managed to acquire a large quantity of powdered banana custard which was served to the boys at every possible opportunity. The excess was such that many, when confronted with the real thing when the war was over, were quite unable to contemplate with any pleasure further exposure to that particular flavour.

The Mall School, Twickenham

In 1939 The Mall was a typical mid-20th-century boys' prep school. It was then owned by a Mrs Thistlethwaite who, following the death of her husband in 1937, had appointed a headmaster, Mr Maurice Ellis.

The School was run from Mrs Thistlethwaite's large house in Twickenham, and, in spite of its proximity to central London, evacuation never seems to have been considered as an option. Throughout the Blitz of 1940 and 1941, and the flying bomb and rocket attacks of 1944, The Mall suffered only the occasional broken window pane, although several surrounding properties were seriously damaged.

An Anderson air-raid shelter was constructed on the School's playing field. This, together with the house's extensive cellars, provided protection from anything other than a direct hit. As soon as the sirens sounded, which was frequently, the boys left whatever they were doing and sought refuge. The cellar was by far the more popular location. The Anderson shelter was permanently damp and lit only by lamps and candles. Attempts to continue lessons in these surroundings were quickly abandoned.

The extraordinary wartime ability to detach oneself from the prospect of imminent death or injury is best summed up by the recollections of one Old Mallian who commented – 'We looked forward to the air raid warning; it was all great fun.'

Although the School stayed put, many boys were removed by their parents to safer locations. By 1944 the number had been halved to a mere 70 pupils. With the exodus of young male teachers to fight the war in one role or another, staffing became a nightmare. But at least the ultimate indignity, in those days, of senior boys being taught by female staff was avoided. This, apparently, would have been evidence of a school in serious decline.

Malvern College

Malvern College survived the trauma of two wartime evacuations.

In September 1939 the College was requisitioned to provide a home for the Admiralty if it became necessary for it to move away from London. With the cooperation of the Duke of Marlborough, and despite enormous difficulties, the college community, numbering some 500, was found a home at Blenheim Palace. The Long Library was converted into a dormitory and lessons were held in the state rooms, with the priceless tapestries on the walls being protected by hardboard. Prefabricated huts were erected in the great quadrangle, and a trench was dug to bring additional gas supplies from Woodstock.

In the event the Admiralty did not move to Malvern, and only three of its ten houses were occupied. One provided a ward room for naval officers, one housed members of the WRNS and the third was used as accommodation for Free French cadets after they had escaped from France.

So after three terms away the College returned home, and the reduced number of boys was accommodated in the remaining seven houses. But by 1942 the south-coast location of the Telecommunications Research Establishment, where radar technology was being developed, was becoming increasingly vulnerable, and Winston Churchill personally ordered its immediate evacuation to Malvern.

The College was required to move again, but by then most suitable premises in safe rural areas had already been occupied. It was only a chance remark that Harrow's numbers had dropped because of its proximity to central London that led to a feasible, if hazardous, solution. The Headmaster and Governors of Harrow generously agreed to house Malvern and provide access to all the School's facilities.

Malvern remained at Harrow until September 1946 when it returned to its own home with 400 boys – a significant improvement on the nadir of 250 recorded in the darkest days of the war.

Back at Malvern the College found that the needs of radar research had transformed its premises. Classrooms had been converted to workshops, the grounds were covered with brick and concrete laboratories and the whole was surrounded by a massive barbed wire fence. Remarkably, the request that the main cricket field should not be built on had been respected. The rehabilitation of the campus was a long and expensive process.

But the radar research and development work that had been carried out at the College during the war made a major contribution towards the achievement of victory. Malvernians like to postulate that, if Waterloo was won on the playing fields of Eton, then the same could be said of the Second World War and the playing fields of Malvern.

Malvern Girls' College

Buildings in Malvern seemed to have been high on the government's requisition list at the beginning of the war, and it wasn't long before the Girls' College was required to vacate its premises and follow Malvern boys into exile.

Attempts to find a new home which could house the whole College were not successful, and the girls were spread around three separate locations in Somerset. Seventy junior girls went to Horsington House. This property, which included 20 acres of land and three cottages, was purchased for £6,000. Another 70 pupils from the Middle School were housed in a rented property at Brymore, and 150 older girls took up residence at Hinton House, near Hinton St George.

However, the government decided quite quickly that it did not need to retain possession of the College's own buildings in Malvern, so the brief evacuation came to an end with a return home in 1940.

Margate College

The College's building was requisitioned in November 1939 and shortly afterwards was completely destroyed by enemy action.

The small number of remaining pupils were accommodated at Willingdon School, Eastbourne and Clifton School, Margate.

Margate College never reopened.

Marlborough College, Wiltshire

The College hosted City of London School from 1939 to 1944. Marlborough used its classrooms during the mornings and City of London boys took over in the afternoons.

Mercers' School, London

The School departed from its central London premises in September 1939 and travelled to Horsham where it joined up with Collyers' School, also run by the Mercers' Company.

By the following Christmas the inactivity of the Phoney War persuaded the School that it was safe to return to London. The return was short-lived. In September 1940, as the bombs began to fall, Mercers' made its second excursion to Horsham.

The School remained there until 1942 when once more it travelled back to London. This time the parents of some pupils questioned the wisdom of the move, and a number of Mercers' boys remained at Collyers'.

Merchant Taylors' School, Crosby, Liverpool

The School did not evacuate in spite of the heavy bombing of Liverpool, and managed to survive unscathed.

Merchant Taylors' School for Girls, Crosby, Liverpool

The Girls' School also stayed in Liverpool throughout the war.

During air raids lessons were frequently taken in the shelters that had been built on the playing fields, and hockey matches took place on the grass that remained between the shelters.

Merchant Taylors' School, Northwood, Middlesex

Situated only a few miles from central London, Merchant Taylors' could have expected evacuation to be mandatory. But the School had moved into newly built premises in 1933, and these included a network of modern underground service tunnels which were lined with concrete. In 1938 Home Office officials deemed that these were suitable for use as air-raid shelters, and Merchant Taylors' remained at Northwood throughout the war.

By 1940 the tunnels were in regular use as warnings of raids became increasingly frequent. In spite of heavy attacks on the area the School's buildings remained relatively undamaged. A stick of bombs which fell across the river shattered some windows, two incendiaries fell harmlessly in the grounds and the roof was sometimes peppered by shrapnel from overhead dogfights, but otherwise the School survived intact.

As early as 1938 Merchant Taylors' had decided to offer day boys the option of living at the School should hostilities break out. A year later many parents decided to take up this offer and, at the start of the Autumn Term in 1939, 90 boys arrived carrying a diverse assortment of bedding ready to become 'emergency boarders'. The group was formed into a 'shadow' boarding house, and the majority were accommodated, at least initially, in the Examination Hall, with its heavily sandbagged windows. The routine of school life quickly adapted to this new arrangement, and the emergency boarding scheme operated for the next four years.

It is perhaps surprising that the School's buildings were never requisitioned. At different stages of the war the authorities considered using them as billets for troops, an emergency hospital and then a public health laboratory. It was even suggested that, in the event of an invasion, the playing fields should be filled with sheep and cattle evacuated from East Anglia. But none of these proposals came to fruition.

Nevertheless, the School was not immune from England's determination to defend itself against the anticipated arrival of the German army. Three pillboxes were built in the grounds, trenches and anti-tank ditches were dug and a concrete machine gun post was constructed over the porch of the Great Hall.

Staff and senior boys quickly became involved in civil defence duties. The roof of the Great Hall became an important lookout post from where one unfortunate Old Boy, acting as an air raid warden, reported a bomb falling on Rickmansworth, only to discover subsequently that it had destroyed his own house.

The School formed a Home Guard unit which indulged enthusiastically in training exercises at weekends. On one occasion its mission was to act as an enemy section trying to capture the airfield at Northolt. To everyone's surprise the operation was successful, and the War Office had to ask for the RAF base to be returned.

Millfield School, Street, Somerset

Early in the war Millfield's Headmaster, Mr R.J.O. Meyer, offered accommodation to his own old school, Haileybury, but in the event Haileybury decided to remain at its Hertfordshire home.

In 1943 Millfield did take in a small number of boys from Eastman's School. This Burnham-on-Sea prep school had evacuated to Trefriw in north Wales at the beginning of the war. Pupil numbers there dwindled to the point at which the school was no longer sustainable on its own, and the remaining boys were absorbed into Millfield. Eastman's Headmaster, Mr Victor Edghill, became joint Headmaster of Millfield prep school in 1945.

Mill Hill School, London

The proximity of the School to Hendon airfield and the barracks of the Middlesex Regiment was sufficient to convince Mill Hill that an early evacuation was unavoidable.

The School travelled north from London in September 1939 to move in with its chosen host, St Bees in Cumbria, while the prep school went to Cockermouth. Mill Hill did not return to London until the summer of 1945, and its buildings were used as a hospital during the war years.

St Bees' facilities were shared by the two schools, although each retained its own teaching staff and boarding accommodation.

Many exiled Millhillians enjoyed exploring the beautiful Cumbrian countryside and coastline. Sometimes the explorations became rather too daring, and on one occasion an over enthusiastic group of boys managed to become cut off by the tide and had to be rescued by the local coastguard – an incident that perhaps achieved more attention than it deserved when it was headlined in the following day's *Daily Mirror*.

But many of those who spent the majority of their Mill Hill years at St Bees describe their stay there as 'the best time of their lives'.

Milton Mount College, Crawley, Sussex

Towards the end of the Summer Term in 1940 Milton Mount was advised that its building in Worth Park was required for army purposes. The College was given one week to vacate the premises.

A long search for an alternative home eventually ended at the *Imperial Hotel*, Lynton in Devon where the College reopened the following September. The staff and pupils settled into their new West Country environment and during the war years formed strong links with Badminton School from Bristol, which had taken up residence at the *Tors Hotel* in nearby Lynmouth. The two schools organised many sporting events with one another, and jointly arranged a variety of lectures and concerts.

The College's own home in Sussex was eventually released by the War Office in June 1945, but the building was in such a dilapidated state after a long period of occupation by Canadian troops that it took almost a year to restore it to a satisfactory condition.

Milton Mount eventually reopened in its original home on 1 May 1946. But the development of Gatwick Airport and Crawley New Town made post-war life increasingly difficult, and the College closed its doors for the last time in July 1960.

The Mount School, York

Although the City of York was not high on the list of Germany's anticipated targets, The Mount School decided to take no chances and opted for evacuation to a more rural location. Cober Hill, a guest house and conference centre six miles from Scarborough, was chosen to be its new home.

The evacuation was short-lived. Cober Hill's facilities were barely adequate for sustaining the life of the School, with pupils having to travel into Scarborough for science lessons in the labs of the Girls' High School. The inconveniences of life at Cober Hill, combined with the realisation that a location on the east coast of England could be even more vulnerable than York in the event of a German invasion, persuaded The Mount to return home after only two terms away.

The Mount School remained in York for the rest of the war.

Newcastle-under-Lyme School (Formerly Newcastle High School and Orme Girls' School)

Adjacent shelters provided safe accommodation during air raids. The Cadet Force became proficient on the rifle range, and many pupils contributed to the war effort during summer farming camps.

Newcastle-upon-Tyne Church High School

The High School's decision to evacuate was partly prompted by a request from Newcastle's Director of Education. He was anxious to communicate the need for evacuation to local state schools, and asked the High School to set an example and lead the way.

The School duly departed for Alnwick in September 1939. At first girls were billeted wherever accommodation could be found for them, but eventually the School established itself with full boarding facilities in Alnwick Castle.

Back in Newcastle the High School buildings were occupied first of all by the ARP, then the police and finally the Ministry of Labour.

The High School eventually reclaimed its buildings and returned from exile in 1944.

New Hall School, Chelmsford, Essex

The dangers of remaining in Chelmsford, between London and the east coast, were considered to be too great, and the search for a new home was started. A suitable property big enough to house the whole School was eventually found in the tiny village of Newnham Paddox in Warwickshire, to the west of Lutterworth.

The School's judgement that evacuation from Chelmsford was essential proved to be tragically accurate. Once New Hall had departed from its own buildings they were requisitioned and used as accommodation to house elderly refugees from central London. The property subsequently suffered a direct hit during an air raid, and several of the temporary residents were killed.

Nottingham High School

The relief that followed the apparently successful conclusion of the Munich crisis in September 1938 was short-lived. By the spring of 1939 war once more seemed inevitable and appropriate preparations were being put in hand across the country. Mr Reynolds, the Headmaster of Nottingham High School, was advised by the authorities that his School lay within an 'evacuation area' and he must make plans to move to a safer location. The School in fact lay in relatively rural surroundings outside the centre of the city, and Reynolds felt the trauma of uprooting the whole School would be greater than the risks of a possible attack from the air. He travelled to Whitehall – along with the like-minded Headmistress of the Girls' High School – to seek exemption from the evacuation directive, but was confronted by a Board of Education who refused to change the rules.

A long and frustrating search for a new home had still not delivered a solution by the time war broke out. At the last minute the authorities relented and telephoned to say that the School could remain in Nottingham. Unfortunately before this news could be passed on to the local billeting officer, he had already assigned the School's buildings to a battery of the South Notts Hussars. A compromise was eventually agreed with the army occupying the newly built West Block – which had only been in use for half a term – and the dining hall – which also had recently been refurbished and

1 *Bomb damage at Clifton College, November 1940.*

2 *Evacuation was not always a hardship. The girls of Commonweal Lodge in Devon.*

3 *Croham Hurst School moved from its surburban London home to the very different surroundings of Bridge House at South Petherton in Somerset.*

4 *Air-raid shelters in the grounds of Ipswich School.*

5 *The aftermath of a flying bomb attack on Croydon High School in 1944. From an original by a pupil.*

6 *Kent College evacuated from Canterbury to Truro. Here the Headmaster of Kent College leads the Truro School Air Training Corps on a parade through the town.*

7 *Kingswood School's Hall becomes a department of the Admiralty.*

8 *Like many others, the boys of Lord Wandsworth College regularly helped out the local farming community.*

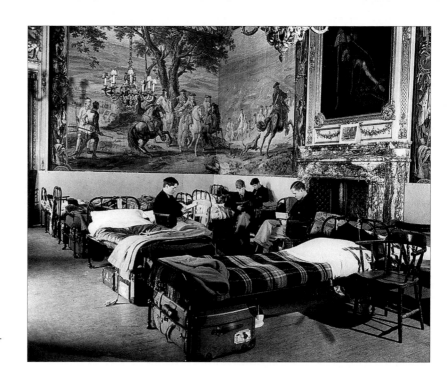

9 *The stately rooms of Blenheim Palace provided a rather different décor for Malvern's dormitories.*

10 *Morning PT in front of Blenheim's familiar façade.*

11 *Lancing's premises became a Royal Navy establishment titled HMS* King Alfred. *King George VI visited in May 1941.*

12 *Joyful chaos as the boys of Portsmouth Grammar School move back into their own home in January 1945.*

13 *Defensive trenches under construction at Radley.*

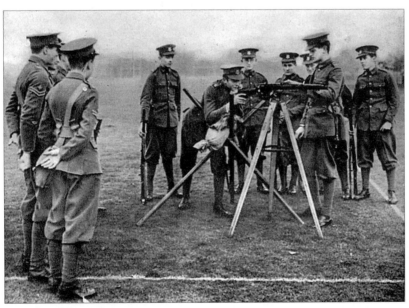

14 *Members of Radley's Corps are instructed in 'musketry'. In 1940 echoes of the First World War were still very much in evidence*

15 *Miss Walpole,*
Headmistress of Red
Maids' School, relaxes after
supervising the sand- bagging
of the buildings.

16 *A lesson in goose*
management for the boys of
King Edward's, Five Ways.

17 *The boys of St Lawrence College, Ramsgate, man their namesake steam engine at Victoria Station in January 1946 before starting their triumphal return journey to Kent.*

18 *In 1939 the grounds of St Paul's Girls' School became the base for one of London's many barrage balloons.*

19 *The library at Wellington College after an air attack in October 1940.*

20 *A Wellington ARP patrol is briefed before setting off for duty.*

re-equipped. The School remained in possession of the rest of its buildings which were barely adequate for the provision of a full education for its pupils, even though at the start of the war their number had dropped significantly to about 500.

An ingeniously improvised timetable was quickly introduced to make the most of the accommodation still available to the School, but even so in early 1940 an Inspector of Schools expressed the view that Nottingham High School 'took the prize for discomfort'.

The Hussars only remained in the West Block for a short period, but they were followed by a succession of other army units, including at one time the Pioneer Corps, who were believed to be responsible for leaving the bullet holes in the ceiling. It was 1945 before possession of the building was eventually returned to the School.

In addition to problems of accommodation, Nottingham struggled during the war years – as did so many other schools – with an extreme shortage of staff. Younger teachers had progressively been summoned to war service and the remaining senior citizens found themselves resuming responsibilities from which they had previously retired. By 1945 rugby coaching was back in the hands of the gentleman who had previously stood down from the post in 1936, and the cricket team was being run by two over-60-year-olds. Great credit is due to these venerable members of staff for the fact that the School continued to maintain a high standard of sporting success throughout the war years.

Oakham School, Rutland

Oakham appears to have been little affected by the war, but rugby against Kingswood School, which was hosted by Uppingham, became a regular fixture.

Old Palace School of John Whitgift, Croydon

In 1938 Old Palace was beginning to lay plans for the celebration of its Golden Jubilee the following year. Priorities changed rapidly during the summer months and by September war with Germany seemed imminent and the Jubilee had been all but forgotten. Attention was totally focused on whether to evacuate or not. A frantic search for a possible new home was started, and the girls were told to be ready to leave Croydon at 24 hours' notice. Then, suddenly, the news from Munich was good, and everybody relaxed into what turned out to be a false feeling of security.

The euphoria did not last for long. Just under a year later, after the Jubilee had been commemorated in an atmosphere of apprehension and foreboding, evacuation was once more at the top of the agenda. On Monday, 4 September 75 girls – quite a small proportion of the total roll – assembled at the School and marched towards the railway station. Amazingly, neither the girls nor the accompanying staff at this stage knew their destination. It was only when they arrived in the station car park that they learnt they were heading for Eastbourne.

The makeshift arrangements in Eastbourne did not work well. The large house in which most of the girls were billeted was virtually unfurnished, and the allocated teaching accommodation at Eastbourne Technical School was inadequate and unsuitable. With a drastically reduced number of pupils the School also lacked financial viability, and forceful representations to the Board of Education eventually resulted in permission to return to Croydon for the start of the 1940 Spring Term.

Six months later, as mainland Europe succumbed to the German onslaught, a second evacuation was seriously considered – but rejected. Old Palace would stay where it was. Both staff and girls were given the option of leaving for safer parts of the country if they wished, and on 10 June a mere 14 girls attended school. With characteristic British determination in the face of adversity, the house tennis tournament was played as planned the following day.

For the stalwarts who remained, there followed months of almost unimaginable trauma, stress and danger. Croydon suffered badly during the Blitz, and the School soldiered on in spite of shattered windows, fallen ceilings and sometimes complete days spent in claustrophobic air-raid shelters.

Gradually the dangers lessened and hope grew as the war seemed to swing in favour of the Allies during 1942 and 1943. For London and Old Palace it turned out to be yet another false hope. In Croydon the devastation caused by V1 flying bombs in 1944 was actually worse than the Blitz. The School's patched-up buildings suffered further damage, and once again the staff and girls lived with the awful knowledge that death or serious injury could come at any time.

The School survived, and the spirit of the British at war is perhaps exemplified by Old Palace's Founder's Day celebration on 2 October 1944. The ceremony took place in the Banqueting Hall as rain poured in through what was left of the roof.

The Oratory School, Woodcote, Berks

The Oratory decided to move away from the south east and was provided accommodation by another Catholic school, Downside at Stratton-on-the-Fosse in Somerset. The evacuation in fact only lasted for two terms – Michaelmas in 1941 and Lent in 1942.

But the return to Berkshire was to new premises. The School's old building, Caversham House, had been sold, and in early 1942 The Oratory purchased Woodcote House near Reading, where it reopened for business in May that year.

Oundle School, Northamptonshire

Nervous tension prevailed throughout England as war became real on 3 September 1939. The following day a loud bang caused Oundle to believe briefly that it had been the target of an early German air raid, but the noise proved to be nothing more than the town's workhouse chapel being struck by lightning.

Oundle, in the heart of the Northamptonshire countryside, certainly did not feature on the Luftwaffe's list of primary targets. Indeed, the only two occasions on which the area experienced any element of enemy aggression were probably caused by the mistakes of German aircrew rather than any serious intent to do damage. In July 1942 a Heinkel bomber shot off a few rounds at the School, which by then, fortunately, had broken up for the summer holidays. And on another occasion a stray bomb landed on the nearby golf course, killing a horse that had the misfortune to be in the wrong place at the wrong time.

The School suffered little real danger during the war, but nevertheless had to adapt quickly to a world that had abruptly changed beyond all recognition from the relaxed pre-war days of the 1930s.

With the introduction of rationing both the quality and quantity of food declined rapidly. But the School's rural location helped it to redress at least some of the deficiencies. Several senior boys became competent marksmen with air rifles, and local rabbit and pigeon appeared frequently on the menu.

Government campaigns to 'Grow your Own' and 'Dig for Victory' were entered into with enthusiasm. There were ample opportunities for Oundle boys to help out on local farms, especially during the summer holidays when farm camps were arranged. Harvest time was particularly busy with Oundelians quickly becoming competent in the threshing and stacking of wheat and barley. The School also operated its own farm which successfully reared pigs and sheep. Several school houses developed their own specialities with one breeding rabbits and another raising ducks.

One of Oundle's strengths had always been the quality of its education in the fields of engineering and technology. The School possessed a foundry, a machine shop and a woodworking shop – the only ones for some miles around. These facilities were quickly pressed into service to help the war effort. With boys volunteering to work throughout the holidays, the machine shop produced shell casings and firing pins for rifles and guns, while the woodworkers churned out boxes for hand grenades by the thousand.

At last it all came to an end in May 1945 when the pupils of Oundle School, along with the rest of the town, threw themselves into a frenzy of celebration in the Market Place on VE Day. An enormous line of conga dancers snaked its way around the square, and there is little doubt that on that memorable occasion some of the younger Oundelians experienced the effects of intoxicating liquor for the first time.

Penrhos College, Colwyn Bay (merged with Rydal School in 1995 to become Rydal Penrhos)

Just before war was declared the College was advised that its buildings were to be requisitioned to house a department of the Ministry of Food. Fortunately one of the School's Governors was aware that Chatsworth House in Derbyshire was available to house an evacuated school, and it was to there that Penrhos moved in September 1939.

The College returned to Wales at the end of the war.

Pocklington School, York

Pocklington hosted Hymers College from Hull – and 60 years on a friendly rivalry still exists between the two schools.

Polam Hall School, Darlington

The school buildings incorporated extensive cellars which, once reinforced, provided adequate protection from possible air raids, so Polam Hall remained undisturbed throughout the war.

Portsmouth Grammar School

The search for a new home started in the summer of 1939, not helped by the Ministry of Health which was disinclined to provide any real assistance to what was then a Direct Grant school. Expectation of early German bomb attacks on Portsmouth made evacuation unavoidable, and eventually a somewhat reluctant decision was taken to move the School – at least as a short-term measure – to Northwood Park, a Victorian house just north of Winchester. Northwood had at one time been the home of Clayesmore School, but had been unoccupied for several years.

Initial reservations about the suitability of Northwood proved to be well founded. It just about provided enough space for 400 Portsmouth boys to sleep and be fed, but the remaining accommodation was quite inadequate for teaching purposes. When it was discovered that the building's heating system did not work, and was unlikely to in the future, a second move for Portsmouth became inevitable.

A return to the School's own buildings was not possible as they had already been occupied by the navy. So the Headmaster, Mr Stork, turned his attention to Bournemouth as a possible destination. Here a number of hotels and prep schools had closed as the war started, and a variety of premises was available. Initially three buildings were acquired to be used for teaching accommodation, and arrangements were made to billet most of the boys in private houses. A distinctly uncomfortable and unsatisfactory three weeks at Northwood Park came to an end on 22 September as Portsmouth took up residence in Bournemouth.

It was soon decided that the younger boys would fare better in boarding houses supervised by members of staff, rather than being billeted with strangers, so two further empty hotels were rented for this purpose.

Two local schools made their laboratories available for the teaching of science. Organisation of the curriculum across four different locations was complicated, and masters found themselves cycling or taking the bus from one class to the next, and sometimes teaching subjects that they only dimly remembered from their past. In spite of all the difficulties, educational standards were maintained, and Portsmouth boys won a significant number of open awards to Oxford and Cambridge during the war years.

As the inaction of the Phoney War progressed into 1940 there were inevitable thoughts about a possible return to the School's own home. But these were quickly dispelled by the events of the summer months and the bombing of the Headmaster's own house in Penny Street, Portsmouth.

The School's exile during the war years could not have been more different from its previous halcyon existence in its own home. The enthusiastic expectations of one new Portmuthian joining the School in 1942 were based entirely on what he had seen in the School's pre-war prospectus. It took him some time to recover from the shock of Portsmouth's improvised wartime life in Bournemouth.

Princess Helena College, Hitchin, Herts

Several staff returned to the College during the summer holidays in 1939 to prepare it for wartime existence. A frenzy of activity eventually resulted in 279 windows and nine skylights being successfully blacked out – a project that tempted the Headmistress, Miss Prain, to say at evening prayers, 'Darken our lightness, we beseech Thee, good Lord'.

The cellars of the main house were rapidly upgraded, with lighting and heating installed, to provide reasonably comfortable shelter during air raids. Arrangements were made for all the girls to sleep in the main house so they would only have to descend to the cellars and not leave the building when the siren sounded during the night.

Several bombs dropped within the College grounds, but the buildings themselves were undamaged. On one occasion the army had to be called in to deal with an unexploded bomb which had fallen close by. The staff were advised that it would be detonated at a particular time which happened to coincide with the inter-house gym competition. When the moment came the massive explosion shook the house, and also momentarily shook the girls, but with true wartime grit the competition continued as if nothing had happened.

The government's requisitioning authorities perhaps presented a greater danger to the College than did the bombs. In the spring of 1941 the College was given one week's notice of the army's intention to take over its premises. Pleas from the Headmistress and the Governors went unheeded and an evacuation seemed inevitable, until the timely intervention of a severe epidemic of measles. Nearly a third of the school roll was confined to bed, and there was even one suspected case of pneumonia. The prospect of organising a full-scale removal of the College in these circumstances proved too daunting for the requisitioners, and they turned their attentions elsewhere.

In the latter part of 1940 many believed that a German invasion of England was inevitable. The College dutifully prepared its 'Invasion Plan'. A nearby chalk pit was roofed over and converted into a secondary shelter large enough to house everybody. As soon as German troops were sighted the girls would be escorted to the shelter – which came to be known as 'Hitler Hall' – while a German-speaking member of staff would delay the enemy's advance by engaging them in conversation. Other members of staff were assigned the task of stripping the main house of valuables. The girls would then have been divided into groups, according to where they lived, and escorted home. Perhaps it was just as well that the plan was never put to the test.

Maintenance of morale, particularly during the darkest days of the war, was sometimes not easy. Intense personal grief when the news of a lost relative was received was mitigated by the spontaneous outpouring of support and sympathy from friends and staff that wrapped itself around the bereaved. And at all other times the depressions of war were usually submerged in a truly determined mission to find fun and humour in every aspect of school life.

Prior Park College, Bath

The College did not evacuate, in spite of being hit by bombs.

Queen Ethelburga's School, Harrogate

The School was advised early in 1939 that its buildings would be requisitioned by the Ministry of Works should war be declared, so there was reasonable time to plan an evacuation.

Contact was made with Commander and Lady Vyner, the owners of a property called Studley Royal on the Fountains Abbey estate near Ripon, and arrangements were made for the School to move there if necessary.

Queen Ethelburga's duly arrived at Studley Hall in September 1939, and remained there for the next six years.

In 1946, just as the School was contemplating a return to its own home, disaster struck during the Easter holidays. A serious fire broke out at Studley Hall causing considerable damage. The Vyners lost valuable paintings and furniture, and many of the School's possessions were also destroyed, including 18 pianos.

Perhaps the war years had provided lessons in how to triumph over adversity, as Queen Ethelburga's managed to reopen for the Summer Term on 10 May – only a week late.

Queen Margaret's School, York

Perhaps Queen Margaret's holds the record for the longest school evacuation of the war. It was nine-and-a-half-years before the School resettled in a home of its own.

In 1939 Queen Margaret's was in Scarborough. Its buildings there had been damaged in the First World War by shells from two German battle cruisers which had bombarded England's east coast. In spite of this the School decided initially not to evacuate. Air-raid shelters were built, fees were reduced in an attempt to persuade anxious parents not to move their girls away and great efforts were made generally to present an image of business as usual.

But by 1940 the east coast had become an uncomfortable place to be, and an arrangement was made to transfer the girls to the impressive Castle Howard, located several miles inland. During the last days of the Spring Term staff and pupils packed everything into boxes and trunks, which duly arrived at Castle Howard during the Easter holidays 'in haphazard fashion and filthy weather'.

The house and grounds of Queen Margaret's new home were quite spectacular. Endless corridors and grand rooms, filled with priceless works of art and other treasures – but not really suitable for the day-to-day education of a large number of teenage girls.

Nevertheless, compromises and adaptations were made and the School settled into its very different new environment. But not for long. On the night of 9 November 1940 a disastrous fire broke out. The local fire brigades were unable to control the flames until the following day, by which time Castle Howard had suffered serious damage. The girls were sent home not knowing when, or if, their school would reopen. A stalwart effort by many people in fact enabled the Spring Term to be started in the useable parts of the castle at the end of the following January.

In March grumblings over the makeshift arrangements became more subdued when it was learnt that a German landmine had blown out the centre of the School's buildings in Scarborough.

The war changed the patterns, routines and activities of school life. Fruit picking and potato digging frequently replaced organised games, and in their spare time the girls became dedicated knitters of socks, jerseys and scarves for the armed forces and for those who had lost their possessions in air raids. In 1944 alone, 400 woollen items were completed and dispatched.

On 8 May 1945 Queen Margaret's celebrated VE Day as enthusiastically as the rest of the country. The dignity of Castle Howard was perhaps a little jeopardised when its north front was patriotically draped with red cloaks, white science overalls and blue games tunics, but nobody seemed to mind.

Perhaps Queen Margaret's had developed a real attachment to the castle because the School remained there until 1949, when it moved to its present premises in Escrick Park, York.

The Queen's School, Chester

The School had had the foresight to build three air-raid shelters before the war started, and were therefore able to act as hosts for six months to 250 girls from St Edmund's College, Liverpool while their own shelters were being built.

The two schools shared Queen's facilities. The hosts used the classrooms in the mornings and had games and leisure activities in the afternoon, while the visitors from St Edmund's arranged their timetable in reverse.

The School never suffered from enemy action, but did nevertheless mourn the inevitable loss of some of its surrounding features. A beautiful shrubbery in the grounds which bordered a railway line was cut down 'to prevent the line from being sabotaged'. And the historic iron railings which surrounded the front garden were uprooted and carried away, in spite of vigorous protests, to be melted down and used in the manufacture of munitions.

There were few items that weren't in short supply as the war lengthened, and new tennis balls were almost impossible to come by. The girls' determination to continue playing one of their favourite sports was recognised and supported by Dunlop who arranged to re-inflate old balls so that they could be recycled.

Queenswood School, Hatfield, Herts

Only 20 miles away from central London, Queenswood might well have expected to see some wartime action. It did. During the Blitz 38 bombs fell on the surrounding estate, including one 1,000-pounder which in October 1940 obliterated the hockey pitch, which was only a hundred yards away from the dining room where the girls were having supper. No serious casualties were reported.

Radley College, Abingdon, Oxfordshire

Radley generously shared its facilities with a variety of people and organisations during the war years.

First to arrive, somewhat unexpectedly, was a group of children and expectant mothers from east London, whom the Warden (Headmaster) had found homeless and brought to the College so that it could provide them with temporary shelter.

The next guests were the boys of Colet Court preparatory school. They had been evacuated from their home in Hammersmith to unsuitable accommodation near to the College, and again Radley did not hesitate to make its facilities available to the prep school while it organised a more long-term solution to its problems.

The arrival of 100 boys from Colet Court raised the total number at Radley to over 500 pupils. Accommodating, feeding and teaching such a large number of boys required imagination, detailed planning and abundant tolerance from all concerned.

In fact, Colet Court only remained at the College for a term. The departure of the prep school certainly eased the problems of overcrowding, but with Radley no longer having hosting responsibilities its buildings once more became a possible target for requisition. The arrival in June 1940 of some 150 boys from Eastbourne College was therefore something of a mixed blessing. The problems of overcrowding were back, but the fear of Radley losing its buildings was removed.

During the summer holidays a further contingent arrived from Eastbourne, and at the beginning of the Autumn Term the total of boys to be educated had risen to 600. A bold decision was taken to run the College as a single school with Radleians and Eastbournians merged together, and teaching organised on the basis of a common timetable. The scheme worked perhaps better than anybody expected. The staff of the two Colleges blended well with one another, and there was little acrimony or misplaced rivalry from the boys.

Differences in the boys' uniforms – given Radley's tradition of stiff collars, surplices and gowns – might have perpetuated a 'them and us' atmosphere between the two establishments, but wartime shortages soon put an end to any attempts to preserve pre-war standards. By 1941 compulsory uniforms had been abandoned by both colleges, and boys were allowed to wear any clothes they could lay their hands on. In winter months, with the buildings only being heated spasmodically, woollen jerseys and mufflers became important wardrobe items.

Radley finally bade farewell to the last of its guests from Eastbourne at the end of the Summer Term 1945. On the final night of that term a military band concert was held to commemorate the union of the two colleges which had lasted for five years. In difficult circumstances, the determination of the two Headmasters and the goodwill of the staff and the boys had forged a bond which is still remembered warmly today.

Ratcliffe College, Leicester

Although not far from the towns of Derby, Nottingham and Leicester – all likely targets for German attacks – the College's location, surrounded by countryside, was considered to be relatively safe.

The provision of air-raid shelters was nevertheless mandatory, and the College was fortunate in this respect as it had beneath its playing fields two huge underground storage tanks. It seems that in the early 20th century these had been used to hold the College's gas supply, but by 1939 they contained 70,000 gallons of water. The tanks were duly drained and fitted out as shelters with very basic facilities. They were described as 'cold, clammy, dimly lit by oil lamps and very uncomfortable', and in fact they were only used during the early months of the war. Thereafter, the boys would take to mattresses in the corridors and cloisters when air-raid warnings sounded.

The College's rural location might actually not have been so safe as originally assumed because it lay adjacent to Ratcliffe aerodrome. This was a site used extensively during the war by the Air Transport Auxiliary as a temporary base for brand new aircraft which were about to be flown into active service. It is surprising, therefore, that it was not the subject of enemy attacks. But the proximity of such a diversity of new planes inevitably excited the boys, even if it didn't excite the Germans, and all College activities associated with the air and flying had enthusiastic followings. The Air Training Corps, formed in 1941, was very popular, as was the 'Aircraft Spotters Club' whose members became adept at identifying any aeroplane of any nationality.

In 1945 the announcement of victory in Europe coincided with the Catholic College's annual retreat – a period of prayer and meditation. In keeping with its tradition and ethos, the retreat continued its ordered course uninterrupted. The following day could not have been more different as the College indulged in a raucous and high-spirited celebration.

The Red Maids' School, Bristol

In spite of the School's close proximity to the aircraft factories at Filton, any suggestions that Red Maids' should evacuate were resolutely spurned. And as the award of a place at Red Maids' was such a prestigious achievement, very few girls were withdrawn by their parents. One Red Maid of the time remembers her parents insisting that she should remain at the School, in spite of the dangers, although they had no hesitation in evacuating her sister who attended another school. She remembers cycling to School across the Downs amidst the still smouldering wreckage of the previous night's raids.

The start of the Autumn Term in 1939 was delayed while the School's cellars were strengthened, and trenches were dug in the grounds to provide additional air-raid protection. Trips to the shelters, both during the day, and at night for the boarders, became regular occurrences, and were considered to be an exciting novelty. There was even disappointment when the all-clear heralded a return to the dormitories.

The School quickly settled into its wartime existence, and a 'spare' lesson was timetabled at the end of each day which was used to catch up on whatever subjects had been interrupted earlier by air raids.

Shortages of almost everything meant that compromises and sacrifices had to be made, and the bright red material of the School's distinctive uniform soon became impossible to find. Many of the girls ended the war in very short skirts with very large patches.

The decision not to evacuate Red Maids' was a bold one, but in spite of heavy bombing all around, and incendiaries frequently falling on the roof, the School and its staff and girls survived the war relatively unscathed.

Reed's School, Cobham, Surrey

Before the war the School was located close to Watford Junction railway station and was therefore unlikely to escape German bombing raids.

So in 1940 plans were made to move Reed's to Totnes in Devon.

The School did return to the south east after the war, but to a new location in Cobham.

Rendcomb College, Cirencester

In the early years of the war troops sometimes camped overnight in the College grounds, and occasionally in the buildings themselves if the weather was bad. But it was 1943 before the requisition of Rendcomb's premises became a serious possibility. In the months before D-Day, England became the temporary home for hundreds of thousands of American service men and women. Rendcomb was considered as a base but rejected because it had poor access for heavy vehicles. Nevertheless, a division of US army engineers took up residence in the grounds, leaving as a memento a large trench filled with discarded personal effects.

The College joined many other organisations in making its contributions to the war effort. Farmers were helped at harvest time, and local fêtes were run to raise money for the manufacture of aeroplanes and warships. It was also a time for self-help. Fuel shortages were mitigated by sawing logs and making briquettes from cement and coal dust, and the meagre food supply was supplemented by wild fruit, produce grown on College allotments and eggs from its flock of hens.

As the threat of air raids became more serious, the College formed its own fire brigade which acquired a portable pump. This was pressed into action on the night in November 1940 when Coventry suffered its worst attack of the war. Several German planes returning from the raid jettisoned high explosive and incendiary bombs over nearby Woodmancote, and the College firefighters were called on to help put out the blaze.

Rendcomb itself survived the war without damage.

Repton School, Derbyshire

In the Derbyshire countryside, Repton was a sought-after refuge for evacuees during the early years of the war.

First to arrive, in September 1939, were the boys of King Edward's School, Birmingham. They remained for the whole of the school year, but the inactivity of the Phoney War persuaded the Governors in the summer of 1940 that a return to Birmingham was appropriate.

The departure of King Edward's was followed swiftly, on 6 August 1940, by the arrival of 100 boarders from Framlingham. It only took two weeks for the Framlinghamians to decide that Repton's proximity to Derby – which had suddenly become a primary target for enemy bombs – was more dangerous than their own east-coast location, and they returned home before the end of the month.

Later in the war Repton maintained its tradition of helping those in need by taking in a group of pupils who had been evacuated from Switzerland.

Roedean School, Brighton

The School's beautiful location on chalk cliffs overlooking the English Channel – such an advantage in pre-war Britain – quickly became a disadvantage as, across the water, Hitler's forces prepared for invasion.

Evacuation became inevitable. The first girls to leave were taking no chances. In June 1940 a group of 50 departed on a 3,000-mile journey across the Atlantic to join Edgehill School in Windsor, Nova Scotia, Canada.

During the following summer holidays the remainder of the School, some 260 girls and staff, travelled north to take possession of three vacant hotels in Keswick in the Lake District. This was to be Roedean's home for the rest of the war.

In April 1941 the School's buildings in Brighton were requisitioned by the Admiralty and became HMS *Vernon*, a shore-based establishment which trained navy personnel in torpedoes and mines.

Roedean began to reclaim its premises in November 1945, and eventually reopened in January 1946.

Royal Grammar School, Guildford

The School remained in Guildford throughout the war.

Parents seeking safer places to continue their sons' education withdrew a number of boys in the early months of the war, but these departures were made up by the arrival of a number of evacuees from the high-risk areas of central London.

Royal Masonic School, Rickmansworth, London

The senior school did not evacuate, and the junior school which had previously been based at Weybridge joined the seniors at Rickmansworth for the duration of the war.

Royal Naval School, Haslemere, Surrey (now the Royal School)

When the war started The Royal Naval School was based at Twickenham, west of London, and it was decided to move to a location further away from the main danger zone.

The School's strong connections with the navy proved to be an advantage, and the Admiralty offered it a lease on Verdley Place in Fernhurst, West Sussex. The evacuation took place on 30 September 1940, and shortly afterwards the School's buildings in Twickenham were seriously damaged by enemy bombs.

Many of the girls had fathers in the Royal Navy and Lord Haw-Haw, Hitler's propagandist, broadcast with supreme cynicism – ' we are sorry to have to bomb the Naval School – so upsetting for the fathers at sea'.

In April 1942 the School moved a few miles north to Stoatley Hall at Haslemere, which is still its home today.

Rugby School

Rugby did not move during the war but had to hand over two of its boarding houses for use by government departments.

Rydal School, Colwyn Bay (merged with Penrhos College in 1995 to become Rydal Penrhos)

The Ministry of Food requisitioned several buildings in Colwyn Bay as the war started, and Rydal School did not escape.

The *Oakwood Park Hotel* in nearby Conway became the School's new home. Its extensive grounds were particularly useful for sports and games.

Rydal was able to return to its own premises in September 1946, at which point its preparatory school moved into *Oakwood Park*, and remained there until 1953.

St Albans High School

The School hosted some sixth-form scientists from Parliament Hill High School for a time.

St Andrew's School, Eastbourne

The School evacuated to Chaddleworth in Berkshire, returning home at the end of the war.

St Bees School, Cumbria

Hosted Mill Hill School

St Catherine's School, Bramley, Surrey

St Catherine's took in about 50 girls from St Mary's Hall School, Brighton in September 1940 when their school was so badly damaged by bombs that it had to close.

St David's School, Purley

St David's was ready for evacuation in 1938. The Headmistress, Millicent Bailey, had arranged to move to a large house in Charlbury, near Oxford. As the news from Europe became increasingly ominous the School began to prepare for departure. Then suddenly the crisis was over and everybody relaxed.

The following August Miss Bailey decided to holiday in the remotest parts of the Scottish Highlands, and chose not to buy a newspaper for two weeks. She returned from holiday to a world that was very different from the one she had left. The School once again hurriedly prepared for evacuation, and this time there was no last-minute reprieve.

Upton Wold Farm in the Cotswolds had by now replaced the house in Charlbury as the destination to which they would escape. It was a lovely old Elizabethan building set in 450 acres of farm land. The bachelor farmer used only a small part of the rambling house, and was happy for St David's to occupy the rest.

Although most parents decided that their children should be evacuated with the School, a small number opted to remain in Purley. So for four years St David's operated from two bases nearly 100 miles apart, with staff alternating between the two locations.

At Upton Wold the children revelled in life on a working farm. Horse-riding became a popular pastime, and the arrival of new lambs, calves, kittens and a foal were greeted with wonder and delight. For the Headmistress and staff life on the farm was not quite so idyllic. The heating was far from adequate, the roof wasn't very good at keeping out rain and melting snow, and when colds, flu, German measles and an appendicitis struck the local medical services were found to be a bit basic.

By the autumn of 1940 the Purley branch was in the thick of the Blitz and yet, ironically, it was Upton Wold which suffered the first near miss when a stray German bomber jettisoned its load of high explosives in the nearby countryside.

As the situation on the home front gradually began to improve, numbers at Upton Wold dwindled and in 1943 the 'country branch' of St David's was closed and the remaining pupils moved back to Purley. But turmoil returned the following year as Hitler's flying bombs began to descend on London. In the space of a fortnight in June three hits very close to the School caused substantial damage. With no windows or doors, collapsed ceilings and a tileless roof, closure was inevitable, and the summer holidays started early. But by mid-September the building had been patched up and St David's opened for the Autumn Term with an increased number of pupils.

St Edmund's School, Canterbury

Canterbury was close to the Kent beaches that could well have been used as the landing grounds for an invading German army, and by 1940 evacuation was essential. King's School Canterbury had already taken the decision to travel west, to St Austell in Cornwall, and St Edmund's decided to follow suit, and in fact teamed up with them.

King's and St Edmund's seniors were based in the *Carlyon Bay Hotel*, while the juniors were close by in the *Bayfordbury Hotel* (since renamed the *Cliff Head Hotel*).

In St Edmund's absence its buildings were used by the army as a field hospital.

The School resettled in Canterbury after the war, and plaques have recently been erected in both the two Cornish hotels to commemorate the evacuation.

St Edward's School, Oxford

The Headmaster, Warden Henry Kendall, was keen that St Edward's should make every effort to help other schools in more vulnerable parts of the country, and he wrote to three preparatory schools on the south coast offering to provide them with accommodation and facilities should they decide to evacuate.

St Bede's Preparatory School in Eastbourne gratefully accepted this offer, and in June 1940 travelled to Oxford by train and Southdown bus to take up residence at St Edward's.

Meanwhile the boys of St Edward's were fired with a determination to be prepared for any eventuality the war might throw at them. The Officer Training Corps tripled in size, and 90 senior boys and some members of staff joined the local Home Guard, going out on patrol to watch for parachutists and other suspicious characters. The effectiveness of these exercises might have been a little questionable as on one occasion a patrol slept soundly while around them a tented camp was erected in the School grounds to house refugees from Dunkirk.

St Bede's remained at Oxford for five years before returning to Eastbourne, and over 30 boys from the prep school completed their secondary education at St Edward's.

St Felix School, Southwold, Suffolk

The dangers of an east-coast location, combined with the requisitioning of the School's buildings by the navy, made evacuation inevitable.

A first move to Tintagel in Cornwall was quickly followed by a second to Somerset where St Felix took over Hinton House near the village of Hinton St George. In 1940 this vast baronial hall had recently been vacated following a brief occupation by Malvern Girls' School. The condition of the buildings was far from perfect, providing a variety of headaches for the staff, but the grounds, full of cedar trees, were beautiful and much enjoyed by the girls. The sunken garden provided an ideal setting for Shakespearean performances during the summer months.

One legacy of Malvern Girls' stay was some hastily erected and rather basically constructed washing facilities which became known as the Malvern Bathrooms. The insides of the baths themselves sported a distinctive black line which indicated the maximum permitted water level.

St George's College, Weybridge, Surrey

Some pupils from local state schools were accommodated by St George's during the war.

St Helen's School, Northwood, Middlesex

The Headmistress had prepared a wartime contingency plan well in advance and in September 1939 the boarders were packed off to Tregoyd, near Hay on Wye, in Wales.

It had been decided that the day girls would remain at Northwood, and only a few were withdrawn as war was declared. The School's boarding houses were taken over by the Irish Guards, but the day school continued to operate, surviving both the Blitz and the flying bombs. Indeed, pupil numbers at Northwood increased during the war, while the number of girls in exile at Tregoyd gradually declined. The remaining boarders eventually returned home to Northwood in the autumn of 1945.

St James's School, West Malvern, Worcestershire

The spate of requisitioning that required the two Colleges in the centre of Malvern to give up their buildings for wartime occupation appears not to have spread to the nearby village of West Malvern. St James's was allowed to remain in its own home for the duration of the war relatively undisturbed. There were occasions, however, when the School was asked if the army could borrow its showers for the use of soldiers in nearby transit camps. Fortunately, the shower block could be shut off completely from the rest of the School, and there were no known encounters between showering soldiers and St James's girls.

In the spring of 1940 the ending of the Phoney War was demonstrated all too clearly to St James's when the village of West Malvern became a temporary home for a large number of men recently rescued from Dunkirk. The troops were in a dreadful state, many traumatised, and the staff and senior girls of the School joined the rest of the community in helping them to find accommodation, food and clothing.

But this was the closest St James's came to the realities of war. The night time fire patrols watched the formations of German bombers pass overhead on their way to cause mayhem in cities such as Birmingham and Liverpool, and they watched them return. On the fateful night of 14/15 November 1940 the low clouds to the north were reddened with the reflected glow of Coventry burning below. On one occasion there was brief excitement when an enemy aircraft did crash land nearby, and its crew parachuted down into the arms of the local Home Guard, but otherwise West Malvern failed to attract the attention of Hitler's Luftwaffe.

Nevertheless the girls participated enthusiastically in any activity designed to help the war effort, and worked particularly hard on collecting donations during fund-raising campaigns such as Warship Week and Salute the Soldier. Between 1940 and 1944 the School paid in thousands of pounds at West Malvern post office which as a result topped the league of Worcestershire village post offices.

St John's Preparatory School, Bexhill, Sussex

By June 1940 the danger of living on the south coast seemed to have become so great that the owner of St John's, Miss Hamilton, decided to close the School and send the children home.

A search for a new home during the summer months proved successful, and St John's reopened for the Autumn Term at Warnham Court, just outside Horsham. Its building in Bexhill was taken over by the army.

Ironically, it turned out that it would have been safer for the School to remain on the south coast. In December 1940 the Horsham area suffered a major air raid and Warnham Court's home farm, immediately next to the School, was hit and burned to the ground.

Once again the pupils were sent home and the School closed. Miss Hamilton, who had already reached retirement age, reluctantly decided not to attempt yet another resurrection of the School, and St John's 160-year existence finally came to an end.

Arrangements were made for the pupils to be accommodated in other schools, and about 70 girls moved en bloc to Westonbirt School where they formed the basis of a new preparatory school.

St John's School, Leatherhead, Surrey

For most of the war St John's shared its classrooms and playing fields with the girls of St Martin-in-the-Fields High School. It would seem that the staff of both single sex schools were perhaps unduly apprehensive of the possible problems that could arise from this situation, and great efforts were made to maintain complete segregation between the boys and the girls. At least one Johnian of the time expressed the somewhat regretful view that these arrangements were so successful that even the long-range sighting of a St Martin's girl was a rare event.

St Lawrence College, Ramsgate

An early decision was taken by the College to move away from Ramsgate, and an arrangement was made to move in with Seaford College. It seems strange today that Seaford on the Sussex coast was then considered to be a safer place than Ramsgate.

By the summer of 1940, the dangers of the south coast had become all too apparent. Seaford decided to evacuate, and St Lawrence moved independently to take up residence at the home of Major General Sir Hereward Wake at Courteenhall just south of Northampton.

There the College remained until early 1946. On the morning of 28 January that year Lawrentians gathered on Platform 1 of Victoria station in London to commence a memorable train journey back to Ramsgate. The significance of the occasion was duly recognised by the Southern Railway who arranged for the train to be pulled by the steam engine bearing the nameplate St Lawrence.

St Mary's Hall School, Brighton
The School closed at the beginning of the war, but the determined efforts of the pre-war Headmistress and a group of old girls enabled it to be reopened in 1946.

St Mary's School, Cambridge
During the war the School took in refugees from both Belgium and Malta.

St Mary's School, Wantage, Oxfordshire
For the girls of St Mary's, tucked away in the Oxfordshire countryside, the war had little effect on the routine of school life. The swimming pool was requisitioned to store food for the local population in the event of a serious emergency, and seemed to be filled mainly with tins of biscuits, but otherwise the nuns went to great lengths to ensure that the possible distractions of wartime were kept to a minimum. Even the quality of school meals was somehow maintained at a surprisingly high standard.

The staff realised, however, that the presence of the Cheshire Regiment, stationed in the town, was unlikely to be completely ignored by the senior girls, and eventually the School's gym became converted into a canteen for the soldiers. Dances were organised on Wednesday evenings and there were entertainments organised in the School hall on Saturdays.

St Mary's was little troubled by air raids. Only once did the warning sound in the middle of the night when the girls were disappointed to be confronted by the nuns in their full habits. The burning question of what the sisters wore when they went to bed remained unanswered.

St Paul's School, London
Plans for an evacuation were laid early in 1939. The Marquess of Downshire had offered to make available part of his mansion at Easthampstead Park, near Crowthorne in Berkshire. This would be used to provide basic teaching accommodation, with the boys being billeted in the surrounding area.

A trial run of the evacuation plan was carried out in March, with bicycles being used as the main means of transport.

Six months later the operation was repeated, but this time it was for real. The number of boys pre-registered for evacuation was 350, but this total rapidly rose to 580, stretching to the limits the abilities of those organising billets. The growing demand for accommodation was partly satisfied by the acquisition of a number of empty houses which were converted into hostels, each run by a member of staff.

Most boys continued to use their bicycles to travel between their billets and Easthampstead. The sudden arrival of nearly 600 hundred junior cyclists in the country lanes understandably generated a degree of traffic chaos, and a Cycle Corps consisting of staff and prefects had to be formed to act as a local police force.

The Marquess's mansion was rapidly adapted for school purposes, the ballroom becoming the hall and the dining room being converted into a library. In addition nearby Wellington College made available its science laboratories, and the makeshift arrangements soon became accepted and tolerated as a wartime way of life.

But separated from its own facilities in London, the sporting life of St Paul's struggled to survive. Rugby and cricket matches continued, albeit on very different and much reduced fixture lists, but away from the Thames the rowers of the Boat Club had little opportunity to train or compete. The sports which tended to flourish were those which did not require extensive outdoor facilities. The fencing team performed steadily throughout the war, and the School's boxers achieved many successes.

Back in West Kensington, St Paul's London home was taken over by the army and eventually became the headquarters of one of the School's most famous old boys, Field Marshal Montgomery. From his base in the board room Montgomery planned Operation Overlord, the invasion of Normandy, and on 15 May 1944 the final planning conference and briefing were held in the School's theatre, with senior allied commanders, King George VI and Winston Churchill all present.

A year later, victory in Europe had been achieved and St Paul's was advised that it could return home. But the war had taken its toll. The science block and swimming pool had been damaged by a flying bomb, the library had lost its windows, a fire had gutted the biology laboratory and there were Nissen huts standing on the rugby pitch.

A hectic summer of building work, refurbishment and cleaning, much of it carried out by staff and boys, eventually enabled St Paul's to reopen for the Autumn Term on 1 October with 400 pupils.

St Paul's Girls' School, London

Miss Ethel Strudwick, High Mistress of St Paul's Girls' from 1927 to 1948, favoured an evacuation of the whole School to an independent location away from London. But the Governors decided this was not feasible and a search for a host school ended when Wycombe Abbey in Buckinghamshire offered to share its premises with St Paul's.

In fact only a minority of St Paul's girls – 183 out of a total of 450 – actually made the move to High Wycombe in September 1939. Many transferred to schools in other parts of the country, while some went abroad and others chose to remain in London.

At Wycombe the junior forms of the two schools were merged. Senior Paulinas were taught separately by their own staff, but some of the new arrivals found it difficult to acclimatise to the rather conservative ethos of their boarding school host. In London they had had freedom to roam as they liked. At Wycombe Abbey girls were only allowed out, in groups of four, for two hours once a week.

Any frustrations did not last for long. By the spring of 1940 there was pressure for St Paul's to return to London. The decision was taken to reopen the Hammersmith premises for 150 girls in May that year, although 70 remained for a bit longer at Wycombe, and for a term Miss Strudwick shuttled between the two sites.

By the start of the Autumn Term the whole School was reunited in London. Its facilities were somewhat depleted – the swimming pool had been requisitioned by the fire brigade at the beginning of the war, and its playing fields were now in the possession of the Air Ministry – but these were relatively trivial disadvantages compared with the pleasure of being back in its own home.

Of course St Paul's return to London happened to coincide with the start of the Blitz, and on the night of 15 November 1940 the School was bombed. The members of staff on night duty rose to the occasion. They removed incendiary bombs that had fallen on the buildings and grounds using long-handled scoops, and two mistresses, still in their night-gowns topped with overcoats, clambered over the locked school gates, endangering both safety and modesty, to seek help from the local fire brigade.

Thereafter, apart from losing its iron railing and gates to the war effort in 1942, leaving the grounds 'terribly exposed to marauders', the School survived unscathed to the end of the war.

St Stephen's College, Folkestone

St Stephen's College did not evacuate at the beginning of the war, but by the spring of 1940, with Dunkirk only a few miles away across the Channel, the need to move was urgent.

The College sought a new home by placing an advertisement in *The Times*. A response was received from Lady Desborough offering to make available her family home at Taplow Court near Maidenhead.

St Stephen's was extremely grateful for the offer, but found the magnificent house and its surroundings not ideally suited to running a girls' boarding school. The Desboroughs' prize herd of Jersey cows roamed the grounds, and inside the house, which lacked most 20th-century amenities, the walls of the rooms were adorned with the massive heads of animals shot by Lord Desborough in Africa.

But with determination the College adapted successfully to this rather different environment, and for the girls it was a unique and magical place in which to live and learn.

St Stephen's remained at Taplow Court until December 1945, and then moved back to the Kent coast to reopen at Broadstairs in premises that North Foreland Lodge School had used before the war. St Stephen's closed in 1991.

St Swithun's School, Winchester

Initially, St Swithun's took in Atherley School from Southampton, which had been evacuated from its own premises. But this arrangement only lasted for two terms.

By the summer of 1940 St Swithun's main buildings were requisitioned by the Royal Army Medical Corps, and St Swithun's itself had to move. The School already owned several boarding houses in Winchester and, with the acquisition of two further rented properties, it was decided it would be possible to remain close to home, even if it meant operating in a rather fragmented manner.

At first the School was allowed to continue using its playing fields, swimming bath, sanatorium and one laboratory. But in 1942 the RAMC decided it needed all the buildings. They were later handed over to the American Army as a military hospital.

The girls were still allowed to make occasional visits for sports and swimming, and for this purpose they were organised into strict crocodiles, given a military escort and were told that under no circumstances should they look at convalescent soldiers who might be sunbathing in the grounds.

The School was eventually allowed to reclaim its premises in April 1945.

St Teresa's School, Effingham, Surrey

The School suffered one near miss from a bomb which created a crater that became known as the Elephant Pit.

Seaford College, Petworth, Sussex

When war broke out the College still occupied its original home at Seaford on the channel coast. It was soon asked to take in boys from St Lawrence College, Ramsgate, who were being evacuated, but by the summer of 1940 the growing threat of invasion persuaded the college authorities that its own location had become too dangerous, and the decision to leave was taken. Surprisingly, the College chose to move just 20 miles along the coast to Worthing, which did not seem to achieve much reduction in its vulnerability.

Nevertheless, Seaford remained at Worthing until 1946 when it acquired its present home at Lavington Park, Petworth.

Sevenoaks School, Kent

In the Weald of Kent, Sevenoaks might have assumed that it was sufficiently far removed from central London to be out of the main danger zone. Indeed, there are no reports of serious damage to the School, but there is no doubt that it witnessed its fair share of wartime action. In 1940 much of the Battle of Britain was very visible in the summer skies immediately overhead, and four years later V1 flying bombs could be watched chugging their way above the countryside en route to their urban targets.

Contemporary accounts of life at Sevenoaks during the war years give no indications of serious disruptions. The rugby players built up muscle by digging trenches to provide shelters during air raids, and the more horticulturally minded successfully cultivated a variety of vegetables to supplement the meagre food supply. But once the necessary adaptations had been made, school life carried on pretty much as before.

For a time Sevenoaks did provide a home for the evacuated pupils of Shooter's Hill School from south-east London. Sharing facilities between the two schools required some fairly drastic re-organisation of timetables, but the boys soon adapted to such inconveniences as playing rugby on Saturday mornings and continuing with lessons in the afternoons.

The war did provide some boys with new opportunities and experiences. Some were chosen to assist the local Home Guard and learnt how to make Molotov cocktails, a great stock of which were stored to repel invading German forces. In 1944 when fire-watching duties once again became an important part of life, the rotas were organised by the Headmaster, James Higgs-Walker, who participated himself and helped many a sixth former to ward off the cold of the night by generously sharing the bottle of sherry he habitually carried with him.

Higgs-Walker and his wife, Mollie, were determined that the high standards of behaviour and etiquette that they had worked so hard to establish and maintain would not be compromised by a war, and they continued to dress for dinner each evening.

Shebbear College, Devon

Shebbear's location deep in the West Country made it a popular choice for parents wishing to move their sons away from the risks of urban areas.

The College was not required to host a complete school, but received a steady stream of individual evacuees, many of whom stayed on after the war to complete their education. In the late 1940s the school roll was 50 per cent higher than it was in 1939.

When Mr J.B. Morris arrived from Bryanston in 1942 to take over as Headmaster, the Shebbear boys were confronted by a variety of attitudes to the war among the staff. Morris was a jingoistic patriot, but some of the older members of the common room who had had personal experience of action in the First World War viewed the new conflict with more apprehension, and a couple of masters who were confirmed pacifists completed an interesting spectrum of opinion.

Apart from the usual deprivations caused by the shortage of food and fuel, Shebbearians' lives were largely untouched by the war. But perhaps helping with the potato harvest alongside prisoners of war from Italy and Germany gave them some inkling of how other lives had been affected.

Sherborne School, Dorset

Miles away from the main centres of population and industry, Sherborne probably felt quite safe in the home it had occupied for hundreds of years. The School certainly did not expect to be attacked. But war is always capable of generating the unexpected, and one night a stray German aircraft fleeing for home still carrying its load of unused bombs decided to jettison them just as it was approaching the School. The stick straddled the buildings but amazingly fell in open spaces. Nobody was hurt and there was very little damage – but Sherborne would never feel quite so safe again.

Sherborne School for Girls, Dorset

As the war reached its first crisis point in the early summer of 1940 the School decided to offer its girls a radical alternative to staying at Sherborne. Branksome Hall School in Toronto, Canada was willing to provide a refuge for children whose parents felt it would be better if they left the country altogether.

On 26 June a group of 22 Sherborne girls boarded ship and set off across the Atlantic. A further 25 followed in due course establishing a substantial Sherborne community at Branksome Hall, where they were provided with their own boarding house.

The rest of the girls and staff remained at Sherborne throughout the war, and were eventually rejoined by the Canadian exiles.

A strong bond was established between the two schools which, until recently, was recognised by the exchange of one sixth form pupil each year.

Shoreham Grammar School, Sussex (now Shoreham College)

In September 1940 a German invasion of England seemed to be only days away, and Shoreham Grammar, perched right on the south coast between Worthing and Brighton, decided that the time had come to retreat inland. The retreat took them some 30 miles north west to Milland, just south of Liphook.

Milland House was to be the home of Shoreham for the next few years, and although a degree of creativity and ingenuity was required to convert the main house and outbuildings into an educational establishment, Milland proved to be a most satisfactory temporary base.

The house contained many rooms which could be converted into dormitories for small groups of boys, and these were much more popular than the cavernous rooms at Shoreham in which 40 pupils slept together.

A huge barn was large enough to provide teaching accommodation for all forms, and an outbuilding was converted into a science laboratory.

Milland House sat in its own estate of some 400 acres, which itself was surrounded by further countryside. The strict traditional disciplines and routines that were part of the School's culture in its own home were no longer appropriate or enforceable in the new environment. Recognising this the Headmaster and staff gradually and subtly introduced a more relaxed regime, to which the boys responded sensibly, developing their own standards of discipline with commendable success.

The leisure time of the senior boys was enhanced by the fact that the girls of Charters Towers School had been evacuated nearby, which gave them ample opportunity to stretch the newly established principles of self-control to the limit.

Although the School was now removed from the immediate dangers of the coast it was not totally insulated from the fact that England was at war. Bombs dropped on a nearby pig farm, a fighter plane crashed in an adjoining field and in 1944 several V1 doodlebugs, falling short of their London targets, exploded in the area.

The Cadet Force assumed increasing significance in the life of the School, and one or two senior members established a particularly good relationship with some Canadian troops who were based nearby. This eventually yielded an impressive supply of the latest clothing, equipment and armaments for the boys – much to the dismay and frustration of the local, ill-equipped Home Guard unit.

Shrewsbury School
The School hosted Cheltenham College for one year.

Stonyhurst College, Clitheroe, Lancashire
Stonyhurst hosted the English College from Rome for the duration of the war.

Sutton High School, Surrey
Some girls transferred to Sheffield and Nottingham High Schools – both also members of the Girls' Public Day School Trust – but the majority saw out the war at Sutton.

Sutton Valence School, Maidstone, Kent
Sutton Valence claims to be the most easterly school that didn't evacuate, and as a result had spectacular views of the Battle of Britain being fought out over the Weald of Kent.

Taunton School, Somerset
Taunton hosted Eltham College from 1939 to 1945, and the boys of King's School, Rochester joined them in 1940.

The three schools worked particularly closely together, and today there are still old boys of both Eltham and King's who are members of the Old Tauntonians' Association.

Tonbridge School, Kent
Tonbridge hosted Dulwich College for just one term in the autumn of 1939. The task of absorbing 600 Dulwich boys proved to be overwhelming, and the visitors returned to their London home for the start of the Spring Term in 1940.

Tormore School, Deal, Kent
Perched on the Kent coast, Tormore Preparatory School held firm until May 1940, but the events of that month made it quite clear that the time had come to move to a less vulnerable location.

The School's Headmaster, Francis Turner, had become friendly during the First World War with John Chute, the owner of The Vyne, a splendid 16th-century mansion in the heart of the Hampshire countryside. As a possible invasion of Britain became a frighteningly real possibility, Mr Chute had no hesitation in offering his property as a temporary home for the boys and staff of Tormore.

The decision to evacuate was taken on 15 May, and two days later two coaches and one very large van carried Tormore across the country. The boys were bedded down in the Oak Gallery, spending the first night on mattresses surrounded by priceless paintings and sculptures. Teaching accommodation was set up in the Tapestry Room, which at one time had been the parlour of Queen Elizabeth I.

The boys were fascinated by their awesome new surroundings, although slightly disappointed that The Vyne had no claims to a resident ghost. The house was explored and gradually became more familiar, but it was perhaps the 400 acres of grounds, including a lake that was used for both boating and swimming, that caused the most excitement and pleasure. A far cry from the School's modest playing field in Deal.

The boys thoroughly enjoyed the freedom and the different opportunities presented by this splendid rural home, and the warm and caring hospitality of the Chute family, who remained in residence to share their property with Tormore for the duration, just enhanced a wartime experience that is remembered with great fondness by those who were there.

Uppingham School, Rutland

After the Munich crisis in 1938, schools in parts of the country considered to be safe from enemy attack were encouraged to offer to share their facilities with schools which were almost certain to be evacuated. Uppingham fulfilled its duty in this respect, and responded positively to a request for wartime accommodation for the 300 boys of Kingswood School, Bath.

The degree of enforced secrecy that was required of both parties to this arrangement was quite remarkable. War had been declared before Uppingham's Governors were advised that Kingswood School would be arriving within the next few days. Three members of the Board were particularly furious that they had been kept in the dark about this agreement, and attempted, unsuccessfully, to have the decision reversed.

The tension caused by this disagreement was compounded by an extraordinary mistake made by the authorities responsible for evacuations. The girls of Camden High School were supposed to be destined for Bedford, but somehow managed to arrive quite late one evening at Uppingham. Their Headmistress – a determined lady – when learning that the School had empty accommodation, awaiting the arrival of Kingswood, insisted that her girls would not be immediately moved on, and for a couple of weeks Uppingham became co-educational.

The co-habitation of Uppingham and Kingswood for a period of over six years proved to be exceptionally successful, and is still recognised as such by both schools. The extremely different origins and status of the two schools – Uppingham, one of the country's top public schools for the boys of upper-class families, and Kingswood, mainly providing an education for the sons of Methodist ministers – perhaps worked as a positive factor. Two schools with more similar backgrounds would probably have become more competitive with one another, but Kingswood and Uppingham came from totally different worlds, and quickly learnt to live harmoniously together while quietly preserving their own distinctive cultures and traditions.

But two schools could not live in such close proximity without being influenced to some extent by the style of their new found neighbour. Kingswood was interested by Uppingham's dedication to discipline, hierarchy and tradition, but the Kingswood boys actually had a stronger work ethic bred into them. Uppingham excelled at games and the arts, but when it came to the practicalities of staging a theatrical performance, Kingswood's hands-on approach came to the fore.

The rougher edges of the disparity between the schools surfaced only occasionally. Kingswood did once support Rugby School rather ostentatiously during a 1st XV match against Uppingham, and one Kingswood boy, shocked by seeing the Uppingham chaplain pouring sherry one evening, decided to top up the bottle with Worcester sauce. But otherwise the two Headmasters, plus some very committed school captains and prefects, contrived to manage the success of a relationship that would have been difficult to better.

Uppingham's war was not made easier when its Headmaster, John Wolfenden, was put under pressure to take up a temporary senior teaching role for the Air Ministry. For most of 1941 the School was in effect run by an acting Headmaster and, although Wolfenden returned in 1942, it was not long before his final departure to take up the headship of Shrewsbury in 1944.

Walthamstow Hall, Sevenoaks, Kent

As war broke out, the priority was to move children and families away from the major towns and cities, particularly London. Rural Kent was considered to be relatively safe. Nobody anticipated that a year later the Battle of Britain would be fought out in the skies above this south-eastern corner of England, and German bombers would be indiscriminately spraying the countryside with high explosives and incendiaries.

So Walthamstow Hall had made no pre-war plans to evacuate and continued to operate peacefully in Sevenoaks – until the night of 21 September 1940. At about 9 p.m. that night the air-raid sirens sounded. The girls were in any case sleeping on mattresses on the ground floor. Ten minutes later the buildings erupted as one bomb demolished the gym, a stick of 15 incendiaries fell on the science block and a landmine exploded just outside.

Remarkably, no one was killed or even seriously hurt. Contemporary accounts of this event, written by both staff and girls, describe the strange combination of calmness and chaos that immediately followed the bombing. Although the emergency services were quickly on the scene, the buildings were uninhabitable, but temporary billeting arrangements were organised within a couple of hours. The stoicism, and indeed humour, that the girls displayed as, in their pyjamas and dressing gowns, they were organised to spend the rest of the night in strange beds in strange homes exemplifies the spirit of Britain in 1940.

Miss Ramsay, the Headmistress, decided that evacuation was essential at least for the junior boarders and any day girls whose parents wished them to go. After a brief spell at Attingham Park, Pontesford House near Shrewsbury was chosen as the School's new country home, and by November the Shropshire branch was well established with about 45 girls and several members of staff living there.

Miss Ramsay was keen that Pontesford should operate just as another part of Walthamstow Hall, and not become a separate school in its own right. At the end of each school year the eldest girls would say farewell to Pontesford and graduate back to Sevenoaks, where, in patched-up buildings, the senior school continued to operate.

Away from the war, life at Pontesford was idyllic. Surrounded by beautiful countryside, the girls had freedom to roam, and the opportunity to experience rural life, including some of its harsher realities. Vivid accounts of one of the School's pigs being butchered, and the enthusiasm with which 'Peggy' was subsequently devoured as bacon, ham and pies, demonstrated a rapid loss of urban squeamishness.

The Sevenoaks branch of the School managed to survive the rest of the war without sustaining further serious damage. Fire-watching, air-raid warnings and lessons conducted in damp, dark trench shelters became an accepted part of the routine. One external invigilator of a school certificate examination had to order the girls to get under their desks on so many occasions that the whole exam was eventually transferred to one of the shelters.

Pontesford was eventually closed at the end of 1944, and Walthamstow Hall was once again reunited in Sevenoaks.

Wellingborough School, Northamptonshire

Soon after the start of the war Wellingborough offered to provide accommodation for any school wishing to evacuate. Weymouth College was the first to benefit from this offer. The College had reluctantly decided to close at the end of the Spring Term in 1940, and the parents of most of the remaining pupils were happy to accept the proposal that their sons should continue their education at Wellingborough. This contingent was allowed to remain together as a unit in a newly named Weymouth House, with the College's former Second Master, Thomas Nevill as Housemaster.

At about the same time a number of boys arrived from Lynfield School in Hunstanton along with their Headmaster, who actually took over responsibility for the whole of Wellingborough's Junior House.

1940 was not a happy year for Wellingborough. Significant differences of opinion involving the Headmaster, the Governors, the staff, the parents and the old boys escalated to unprecedented levels. This acrimony, combined with the disruptions of a country at war, resulted in a number of boys being withdrawn from the School, and in fact it was only the arrivals from Weymouth and Lynfield that kept Wellingborough financially viable.

The Headmaster, Dr Billen, departed at the end of the Summer Term, and Thomas Nevill, from Weymouth, was appointed to replace him. Nevill set about the tasks of restoring Wellingborough's reputation and increasing pupil numbers. He was successful in both, achieving a rise in the school role from 258 in the summer of 1940 to 310 in 1944. Wellingborough's original policy of opening its doors to evacuees continued to contribute to this growth, not least when it took in a number of boys escaping the aftermath of the devastation of Coventry in December 1940.

The Germans were not particularly interested in the town of Wellingborough. There were a couple of air raids in August 1942, but the School survived both without suffering any damage. It was the American air force which arrived shortly afterwards that gave more rise for concern. They took over two nearby airfields, and presumably were training novice pilots because the number of near misses and actual mid-air collisions became unnerving. After a series of explosions in the sky one quiet sunny morning, one Wellingburian wrote in his diary, 'our American friends are playing bumper cars with their bombers once again!'.

On 8 May 1945 Wellingborough town and School joined the rest of the country in celebrating the end of the war in Europe with enthusiastic abandon. The school chaplain was heard to complain that it was impossible to get a drink in any of the town's pubs that day because there were so many sixth formers in the way.

Wellington College, Crowthorne, Berkshire

The College felt no need to move away from its premises in Crowthorne, and for a large part of the war shared its science laboratories and playing fields with St Paul's who had taken up residence at Easthampstead Park nearby. Also, through the St Paul's connection, it took in the boys of Colet Court for a time, making Wellesley House available for their use.

Nevertheless, Wellington did experience its own wartime tragedy. During an air-raid alert in October 1940, the Headmaster, Robert Longden, had just checked that all the boys were safely in the shelters and was standing outside the Masters' Lodge, when a German bomb exploded almost on top of him. He was killed instantly, although his body was not found until the following day.

Westminster, London

Westminster spent much of the war on the move. Arrangements were made initially with Lancing College, and a trial evacuation was carried out there in 1938. The exercise was repeated a year later, this time for real. Most Westminster boys went to Lancing, but some 90 were accommodated at Hurstpierpoint which was not far away.

Both these south-coast locations seemed to be safe refuges from London in 1939, but by the summer of 1940 they had become distinctly uncomfortable places to be. Although Hurstpierpoint decided not to move, Lancing was preparing to evacuate, and Westminster concluded also that it was time to move on.

The buildings of Exeter University were Westminster's next home, and later in the war a further move was made to Herefordshire.

The frequent moves did not make the School a settled establishment, and the numbers of both day boys and boarders dwindled during the war years to the point at which its very existence was threatened.

Westonbirt School, Tetbury, Gloucestershire

It all happened very quickly. During the summer holidays of 1939 Westonbirt was given very short notice of the Air Ministry's intention to requisition its buildings. At that stage no plans for an evacuation had even been thought about. The search for a new home started, and became even more urgent in the last week of August when 60 Air Ministry staff arrived on the doorstep and started moving in. As the authorities announced that the School's main building must be vacated by 1 September, the Midlands, Somerset and Dorset were all scoured for properties that were both suitable and available. Fortunately the girls were still away enjoying the end of their last peacetime holidays, because it was not until 4 September that two properties were discovered, just eight miles from one another, and only 20 miles from Westonbirt. These were Bowood and Corsham Court. A very rapid removal of the School was organised, and later in September the School opened for the Autumn Term in its new environment.

During the war Westonbirt took in pupils from a number of other schools in more dangerous parts of the country, including a group of some 70 girls from St John's School, Bexhill. Most of these were quite young and it was decided that their arrival justified the setting up of a new preparatory school, which was housed in a third building, Spye Park.

Westonbirt was allowed to return to Tetbury in 1944, even though aircraft were still concealed beneath the trees in the school grounds.

Weymouth College

During 1939 the College was probably more worried about its parlous financial situation than it was about an impending world war. A steady decline in the number of pupils, combined with an overly modest fee structure, had led to a growing burden of debt. When the possibility of an enforced evacuation from Weymouth had to be considered as well – the town was in fact attacked 36 times during the Battle of Britain – hopes of saving the College began to decline.

With great reluctance the Trustees decided in December 1939 that the College would close at the end of the Spring Term. A public announcement was made the following month at the Headmasters' Conference.

The Headmaster of Wellingborough School, Dr Billen, offered to take on any of Weymouth's pupils who wished to transfer. The offer proved popular, and 33 boys, plus Thomas Nevill, the College's second master, who was subsequently to become Head of Wellingborough, made the move. Several of the College's most prized possessions went with them, including items of furniture, library books and cups and trophies. Two years later, the choir stalls from Weymouth's chapel, which had been presented by old boys in memory of those fallen in the First World War, were also installed at Wellingborough.

Whitgift School, South Croydon

Only ten miles from central London, and close to Croydon's international airport, Whitgift lay within a government designated 'evacuation zone'. Initially the School was not allowed to reopen for the 1939 Autumn Term, and in any case many of its pupils and their families were already in the process of departing to less vulnerable locations.

Air-raid shelters were hurriedly built, and as the panic of September gradually subsided, the Board of Education eventually agreed that Whitgift could open for the Autumn Term on 10 October. On that first day less than half of the 800 boys who would otherwise have been at the School actually arrived. But by November, as parents began to believe that the war was not going to be as bad as they had at first feared, daily attendance had reached 500 pupils.

As the anticipated conflict increasingly appeared to be a myth, more boys returned and school life was restored to a semblance of its pre-war routines and activities. But the easing of tension was short-lived. By the spring of 1940 German landings on England's southern and eastern coasts were expected and awaited. There was a renewed exodus from London, and once again the number of boys attending Whitgift was in decline.

But by then the School's air-raid shelters had been improved to a level at which they provided good protection for all pupils and staff, and Whitgift decided to stay put. During the next nine months, as the Battle of Britain raged overhead, it was not uncommon for the boys to spend more of their school day in the shelters than they did in their classrooms. Staff sometimes had to make difficult decisions. If an air-raid warning was still in force as dusk fell during the winter months, should the boys be sent home while there was still a little light, or should they remain in the shelters risking the possibility of a return home in the pitch darkness of the blackout, or, even worse, the prospect of waiting in the shelters all night before they could be released the following morning? Not the sort of responsibility a school teacher would have dreamt he would have to carry a couple of years earlier.

By great good fortune, in spite of being in the midst of the Blitz and also the flying bombs and rockets later in the war, nobody at the School was killed or even seriously injured during the air attacks.

The only direct hit suffered by the School's main buildings was when an incendiary bomb penetrated the roof of the chemistry laboratory, but fortunately failed to ignite. Nevertheless, the Headmaster's house suffered serious damage, and the fives courts were put out of action by a series of incendiary bombs. Shattered windows and fractured roofs became an almost monotonous feature of school life, and before every rugby match the pitch had to be scoured and cleared of shrapnel.

In spite of the traumas of the war years, Whitgift was reasonably successful in maintaining its academic standards throughout, and benefited from a rapid rise in pupil numbers as worldwide peace was restored.

Willington School, Putney, London

At the beginning of the war Willington moved out of London to join up with St Michael's School in Uckfield. But the following year St Michael's premises were requisitioned by the Admiralty, and both schools travelled across the country to take up residence at Tawstock Court, near Barnstaple.

Willington was reopened in Putney in 1941.

Wolverhampton Grammar School

The School was relatively untouched by the war. There was some consternation over the arrival of the first ladies to join the teaching staff, and the School's splendid iron railings were sacrificed to the war effort, not to be replaced until the 1980s.

In 1941, in response to a direct appeal from the government, Wolverhampton set up its own Air Training Corps to help train new pilots who were in such short supply following the losses of the Battle of Britain.

Worth School, Crawley, West Sussex

During the war the School was a preparatory school called Worth Priory which had been founded by Downside School.

In September 1939 the home of Downside near Bath seemed a much safer place to be than Sussex, and it was agreed that Worth should move in with its parent. Worth's buildings were in any case requisitioned. They were used initially by the Canadian army, and subsequently by the 8th British Corps whose commander, Lieutenant General Sir Richard O'Connor, planned his soldiers' role in the D-Day invasion while in residence.

Worth returned to Sussex in September 1945.

Wrekin College, Telford, Shropshire

Far away from the areas likely to be attacked by German bombers, the College nevertheless dutifully prepared for war by organising air-raid precautions, and blacking out all its windows, apart from those of the chapel and the gymnasium which would only be used during daylight hours.

However, the College was not immune from the threat of requisition. At one stage a rumour circulated that all Wrekin's buildings were to be taken over by Somerset House, which was seeking a new home away from London. But by then the College was already doing its bit by providing refuge for a number of evacuated organisations, and as a result managed to avoid being ousted from its own home.

The College's first wartime guest was the Medical Research Council, which set up an emergency public health service in the biology laboratory. The next arrivals were the girls of Smethwick High School, who also shared the labs, working alongside the College's own pupils.

In September 1940 the staff and boys of Hurst Court Preparatory School arrived from Hastings, and stayed until the summer of 1945. They were allocated accommodation in two boarding houses, and had their meals in the cricket pavilion. Hurst Court integrated happily with Wrekin, and the prep school's Headmaster, Mr R.J.S. Curtis, proved particularly useful in refereeing football matches and judging boxing.

Hurst Court proved to be an example of how a well chosen evacuation plan could actually benefit a school. During the five years it spent at Wrekin its number of pupils doubled.

Wychwood School, Oxford

The increasing complacency of the Phoney War was dramatically transformed in the spring of 1940 into an atmosphere of near panic as Holland, Belgium and France fell to the Nazis. A number of Wychwood girls disappeared to new homes in Canada and the USA, and the School itself was offered a house in Pennsylvania. Escape across the Atlantic did not seem to be the right solution, and the offer was rejected. But the number of pupils had dwindled to a level at which the continued existence of Wychwood on its own looked increasingly problematical.

An agreement was reached to work together with Oxford High School, which was itself losing pupils. The majority of Wychwood girls went to the High School for most of their lessons, but girls from both schools attended Wychwood for music and art. Continued use of Wychwood's green uniform helped to preserve the School's separate identity, and every effort was made to maintain its traditions.

These makeshift arrangements were not made easier when one of the Wychwood's main buildings was requisitioned for use by the Ministry of Agriculture, and subsequently made available to the American army.

The army eventually moved out in 1945, and Wychwood set about the task of re-establishing itself in post-war Oxford.

Wycliffe College, Stonehouse, Gloucestershire

On Christmas Day 1938 the Headmaster of Wycliffe, Mr W.A. Sibley, received a confidential letter. It came from the Ministry of Works and advised him that, should war be declared, the College's buildings would be requisitioned.

The search for an alternative home ended when St David's College, Lampeter in Wales offered to make accommodation available. Although St David's was a theological college, it did not expect its students to be exempt from military service and therefore assumed that, in the event of war, its premises would be empty. The authorities subsequently decided that theological students would not be required to enlist, and in September 1939, far from being empty, St David's was still home to nearly 200 budding theologians. At Wycliffe the meteorologists of the Air Ministry were about to take possession, and the College had nowhere else to go. The Principal of St. David's honoured the agreement made previously by his predecessor, who had since died, and handed his buildings over to Wycliffe. Alternative arrangements were made for housing and teaching the St David's students, but for a time there was considerable resentment of the Wycliffe cuckoo which had ejected them from their nest. The antagonism did not last for long. The two colleges quickly learnt that there were advantages to be gained from living in such close proximity to one another, and were soon co-operating with one another on a broad range of activities.

It took Wycliffe a little while to adapt to the different way of life that existed in a small Welsh town. Boys going out on cycle rides on Sunday afternoons were accused of failing to observe the Sabbath. And when the College invited the townspeople to its production of 'The Yeomen of the Guard', there was initially some apprehension at the prospect of going to an 'opera'. The last one in Lampeter had been in 1904. But some imaginative promotion of the production overcame these suspicions, and eventually 1,500 people attended the three performances.

Back at Stonehouse, Wycliffe's buildings never attracted the attention of German bombers, but that is not to say they survived the war unscathed. On 21 November 1939, shortly after the College's departure for Lampeter, a member of staff, who had travelled to Stonehouse for a meeting with the Ministry of Works, spotted a wisp of smoke rising from the chapel roof. In spite of a quick appearance by the fire brigade, the flames took hold, and most of the building was destroyed.

It was as early as June 1940 that Wycliffe opened negotiations to reclaim its own home from the Air Ministry. But it was over five years before the premises were eventually handed back. By 31 August 1945 over 1,000 tons of meteorological equipment had been packed up and moved, and the following day the Ministry staff finally boarded a train and returned to London. The buildings and grounds were barely recognisable from those vacated in 1939, but after a month of intensive restoration and cleaning the College reopened at Stonehouse on 18 October.

Wycombe Abbey School, High Wycombe, Buckinghamshire

As war was declared in September 1939, Headmasters, Headmistresses and Boards of Governors all over England were making decisions about the future of their schools.

Away from London, and with good provision already having been made for air-raid protection, Wycombe Abbey decided that evacuation was not necessary.

It did, however, offer to take in all or part of a school seeking a new home away from the main danger areas, and this resulted in nearly 200 pupils of St Paul's Girls' School arriving to share Wycombe's facilities. But the visitors' stay was quite short-lived, and all the Paulinas had returned to London by the summer of 1940.

By then Wycombe had lost many of its own pupils – removed by anxious parents – and the School's financial situation was beginning to look ominously bleak. In the end it was not a shortage of money but the actions of the requisitioning authorities that determined the School's fate. In March 1942 the Board of Governors were advised that all Wycombe's buildings and grounds were to be taken over by Bomber Command. By then so many other school's had evacuated that finding a suitable alternative home was impossible, and with great reluctance and sadness the decision was taken to close Wycombe. Arrangements were made for the girls' education to be continued at other schools, sometimes in distant parts of the country.

But with the closure came a firm determination that it would be no more than a temporary interruption to the School's life. The Board of Governors remained active and held no fewer than 27 meetings during the four years that Wycombe was closed. The services of the Headmistress, Miss W.M. Crosthwaite, the secretary and bursar were retained, paid for, albeit with difficulty, from the compensation received from the Air Ministry.

In 1944, as the fortunes of war began to favour the Allies, The Governors and Headmistress started to prepare plans for reopening the School. But the reclamation of its premises, which by now had become the headquarters of the Unites States Eighth Air Force, proved to be a painfully protracted process.

With determined but perhaps excessive optimism, applications were accepted for girls to start at a reborn Wycombe in September 1945. It proved to be a false dawn. That summer the Americans were still very much in residence, and it was the beginning of the following year before they finally departed.

In the end it was May 1946 before the School resumed its interrupted life. Wycombe pupils who had spent the last four years of their lives in enforced educational exile at schools such as Malvern Girls', Sherborne and Cheltenham Ladies' College returned to joyful reunions – and Wycombe Abbey rejoiced at its resurrection in an England at peace.

Appendix

The information provided by the schools and old pupils' societies who responded to the AROPS' survey included references to the evacuations and hostings of some other schools.

These references were not researched further, but are included here for interest.

School Name	Location	Notes
Arundel House		Hosted by Kelly College, Tavistock
Atherley	Southampton	Hosted by St Swithun's, Winchester for two terms 1939/40
Avisford (Prep)	Arundel	Hosted by Ampleforth College
Badminton	Bristol	Evacuated to Lynmouth
Barr's Hill	Coventry	Hosted by Leamington High School 1939-40
Carn Brae (Prep)	Bromley, London	Hosted by Cranleigh
City of London Freemen's	Ashtead	Hosted City of London Girls
Claremont (Prep)	Hove	Hosted by Bradfield
Collyers'	Horsham	Hosted Mercers' School
Culford	Bury St Edmunds	Hosted East Anglian School for Girls
Cumnor House (Prep)	Danehill	Cumnor House 2 remained in Danehill after Cumnor House 1 returned to Croydon
Dane Court (Prep)	Pyrford	Hosted by Bryanston
Downe House	Newbury	Hosted Queen's Gate from London
Downsend (Prep)	Leatherhead	Hosted by Hurstpierpoint
Downside	Stratton-on-the-Fosse	Hosted the Oratory School for two terms in 1941/2, and Worth Priory from 1939 to 1945.
Eastbourne High	Eastbourne	Hosted Croydon High,

		Coloma (Croydon), and Notre Dame (Battersea)
Eastman's	Burnham on Sea	Evacuated to Trefriw, Wales. Eastman's closed during the war, with its remaining boys being absorbed into Millfield.
Eltham	London	Hosted by Taunton School
Guernsey State Intermediate	Guernsey	Hosted by Hulme Grammar School, Oldham
Hall	Weybridge	Hosted by Croham Hurst – in South Petherton
Hillsbrow (Prep)	Surrey	Were evacuated to East Anstey, Devon
Hurst Court (Prep)	Hastings	Hosted by Wrekin College 1940-1945
Imperial Service College	Windsor	Merged with Haileybury in 1942
Keighley Girls Grammar	Keighley	Hosted City of London Girls
Keighley Junior Technical	Keighley	Hosted City of London Girls
King's	Canterbury	Evacuated to St Austell, Cornwall
Leelands (Prep)	Deal	Hosted by Benenden
Lichfield	Lichfield	Hosted some boys from King Edward VI Camp Hill School – December 1940 to 1943
Lydgate House	Hunstanton, Norfolk	Evacuated to Ogston Hall, Higham, Derbyshire, which it shared with Downside, Purley
Lynfield	Hunstanton, Norfolk	A number of pupils taken in by Wellingborough School
Monkton Coombe	Monkton Coombe	Hosted Dean Close School (Cheltenham)
Monmouth		Hosted King Edward VI Five Ways School, Birmingham
North Foreland Lodge	Broadstairs	Evacuated to Hook, Hampshire. Closed 1991
Port Regis (Prep)	Shaftesbury	Hosted by Bryanston
Repton	Derbyshire	Hosted Framlingham College (briefly) – and also

		King Edward VI School Birmingham between 1939 and 1940.
Queen's Gate	London	Hosted by Downe House
St Bede's (Prep)	Eastbourne	Hosted by St Edward's, Oxford
St Edmund's	Liverpool	Hosted for six months by Queen's School, Chester
St Faith's	Cambridge	Evacuated to the *Golden Lion Hotel*, Ashburton, Devon
St Martin-in-the-Fields High School for Girls	Tulse Hill, London	Shared the facilities of St John's, Leatherhead
St Michael's	Uckfield	Initially hosted Willington School from Putney. Both schools then moved to Tawstock Court near Barnstaple, where St Michael's still operates today.
Selhurst Grammar	Croydon	Evacuated first to Hove, and then to Bideford Grammar School until 1942.
Shooter's Hill School	London	Hosted by Sevenoaks
Simon Langton Grammar	Canterbury	Hosted Kent College's day boys before evacuating to Wantage itself.
Smethwick High School for Girls	Smethwick	Shared the facilities of Wrekin College
South Hampstead High	South Hampstead	Hosted by Berkhamsted School for Girls
Stoke Park	Coventry	Hosted by Leamington High School 1939-40
Truro	Truro	Hosted Kent College, Canterbury's boarders 1940-45. Playing fields and classrooms were also used by Stoke Damerel Girls' High School, Devonport in 1941.
Victoria College	Jersey	Hosted by Bedford School
Warwick School	Warwick	Hosted King Edward VI Camp Hill School – September 1939 to September 1940.